Jerome L Babe

The South African Diamond Fields

Jerome L Babe

The South African Diamond Fields

ISBN/EAN: 9783743326842

Manufactured in Europe, USA, Canada, Australia, Japa

Cover: Foto ©ninafisch / pixelio.de

Manufactured and distributed by brebook publishing software (www.brebook.com)

Jerome L Babe

The South African Diamond Fields

THE
SOUTH AFRICAN
DIAMOND FIELDS.

BY

J. L. BABE,

SPECIAL CORRESPONDENT OF THE "NEW YORK WORLD."

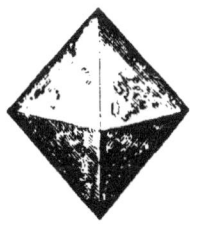

NEW YORK:
PUBLISHED BY DAVID WESLEY & CO
7 & 9 WARREN STREET.
1872.

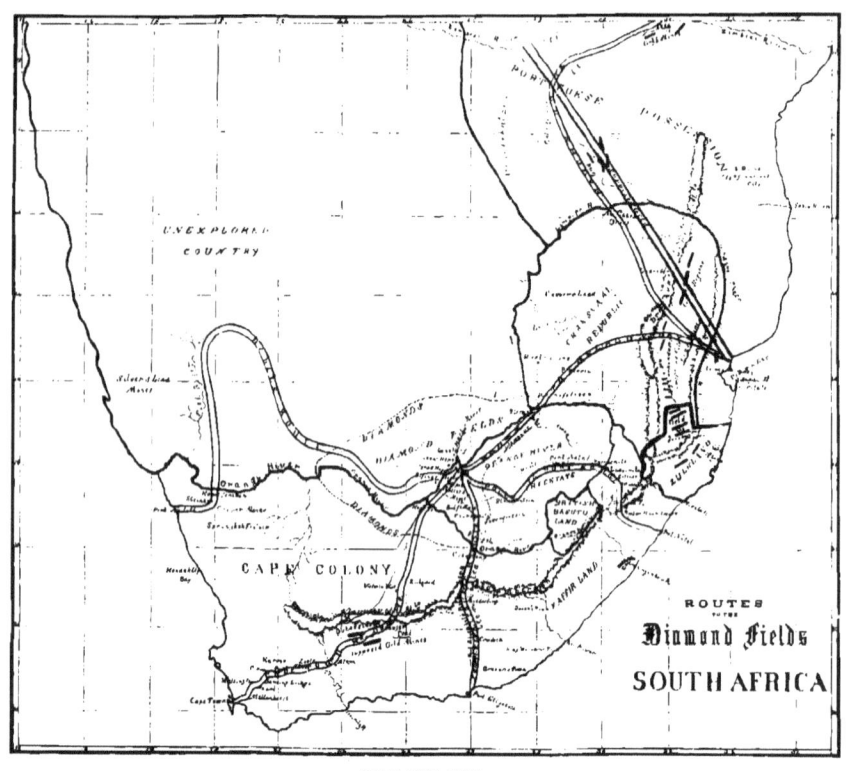

MAP OF SOUTH AFRICA.

INTRODUCTION.

The Diamond Fields of South Africa occupy, at present, the precise position that the gold discoveries of California and Australia did some years ago. Hundreds of emigrants are waiting for reliable information before starting for these fields. Journalists in the Old World and the New have been attracted by the dazzling accounts of the valuable gems that have been found. These finds have been published with all the attractiveness that bold type could give them, but, with the bare announcement, all information has ended, and most of those who have read the news and sighed at the success of the lucky ones, know as little of the land where these fortunes have been picked up, as they do of the interior arrangement of the crater of Vesuvius. It is a very noticeable feature connected with the diamond regions, that the information which has been disseminated through the medium of the press, has, more frequently than otherwise, been unreliable, and in no instance, probably from the fact that in a newspaper sufficient space could not be afforded, has there been published the details which alone could guide those abroad in determining whether it is advisable for them to try their fortune in diamond digging in South Africa. A large number of pamphlets, it is true, have been circulated; but it must be remembered that most, if not all of them, have emanated from those who have some object or other to induce emigration. The writer of this has no interest to serve but that of giving those particulars which he conceives will be of assistance to those whose thoughts are turned toward the Cape Colony in consequence of these diamond discoveries. It is very probable that this pamphlet may have the effect of preventing some men from throwing up comfortable certainties at home to embark in this great diamond lottery; but those who come, after having gone carefully through this work, will, it is certain, be of the right class; and will no more regret their hazard at the fields than the colony will have to mourn over their presence. But it is patent that the pamphlets which have been issued as mere advertising mediums, mere baits to catch emigrants, will do more harm to South Africa than it is possible for any one, at the present stage of the history of the fields, to well calculate. It is not absurd, it is absolutely cruel to bring men to these shores under the delusion that, if they land with £10 in their pockets, they have done the wisest thing possible, and that fortunes they must make. On the other hand, it would be the height of absurdity to warn people that they must not try diamond seeking in this land. To a very large number of persons the best advice that could be given them would be, "start at once;" to probably a very much larger number it would be equally judicious to say, "stay at home and mind the business you are now employed it." This will be best understood from the detailed accounts given hereafter, and the particulars of practical experience at the fields will convey, more clearly than any general remarks, the necessary information to those who are desirous of knowing anything regarding this diamond country. The tales of good fortune and ill success will serve the purpose of conveying the truth better than any comments on the probabilities of finding. There can be no doubt but that these fields open up a new existence for this colony which has, for a long number of years, been unproductive for so vast an extent of land. Colonized by the Dutch two hundred years ago—since then the great half-way house from England to India—having been a wine-producing country for a long period, it has still fallen year by year in the colonial scale of superiority. At one time its vast extent of land gave rise to the hope that it was eminently suited for a wool-producing country. Flocks soon spread over the land, bidding fair to compete in number with that scourge of the Cape, the locusts. Cape wool, for a while, pushed the colony into the stream of prosperity. But then came the *de facto* closing of the United States' market to colonial wool. The wool exports of South America to England increased with marvelous rapidity. Australia, too, surpassed the Cape, and so wool fell in price. The South African wool merchant and the South African sheep farmer had his dream of wealth dispelled like the melting of the morning mists before the rising sun. The flocks are still increasing and wool still pays; but South Africa has learned that upon its wool exports it can not for the future depend for its whole support. Colonists had to turn their attention to other products; and, when all was doubt and uncertainty, when the colonial future appeared at its darkest, the diamond fields burst

INTRODUCTION.

into light like a silver lining to the cloud. For a very considerable while the colonists refused to place any credence in these diamond reports which had reached the ears of the diamond merchants and speculators of Europe. One of the largest of the English firms plausibly, with the intention of setting all doubts to rest, sent, in 1868, a Mr. Gregory to the Cape for the purpose of inspecting and reporting on the probabilities of the existence of diamond mines. Mr. Gregory arrived, made a hurried run through the colony, went no farther than Colesburg, where it was never pretended diamonds had been found, and then returned to his employers with the assertion that Cape diamonds were a myth, a delusion, and a snare. This had the effect of settling for a few months the diamond fever, which had begun to spread throughout the colony; but Mr. Gregory's opinions were very shortly scattered to the winds by the announcement that a farmer named Van Niekerk had taken to Aliwal a diamond which had been purchased by Messrs. Lilienfield Bros. for £11,500. The transition was so great from Gregory to Niekerk that colonists were more credulous than ever. The owners of the gem were, however, well assured of the value of their concession. The "Star of South Africa" was sent to England with all due deference to its importance and value. The report of the diamond buyers at home confirmed the fact that "the Star" was all its owners pretended it was. This intelligence was received with great rejoicing in the country. The colonial press was down on Gregory; and the witticism of the hour, if you desired to tell a man that he had uttered a falsehood, was, that he had told a Gregory. On the receipt of this news the tide of emigration to the Vaal commenced, and has continued to increase ever since. In 1870 the finds were so numerous and so valuable—the exports, too, so large, that the controlers of the diamond markets in Europe could no longer hope to delude themselves or their customers with the belief that there were no such things as diamonds to be found in South Africa. Mr. Costa, of the eminent firm of Costa & Co., of Amsterdam, went post-haste to Capetown and condemned the fields, as far as he was concerned, although not denying the fact that diamonds were being found. He thought it probable that he would return to South Africa if the discoveries were larger. He had hardly left before the finds increased marvelously on what they had been before. The diggers were of a different stamp to those who had been at work previously; they had better machinery, hence their success. This brings us up to the end of 1869, and we then find some hundreds of men at the diggings. During the next year the numbers increased from hundreds to thousands, and now from all parts of the world people are making tracks for the Vaal—with what chance of success the particulars given elsewhere will best explain.

The following note from Mr. D. G. Croly, of the New York WORLD, tells its own story:—

WORLD OFFICE, *March*, 15, 1872.

J. L. BABE—*Dear Sir:* During the temporary absence of Mr. Manton Marble, the editor-in-chief of the New York WORLD, you ask me for some testimony as to your trustworthiness. I can only say that I have known you as a correspondent of the WORLD from South Africa for the past two years, and that so far as my personal knowledge extends, your statements can be implicitly relied upon. You were the first to inform the American public of the very great value of the South African Diamond Mines, and subsequent accounts have fully confirmed all you had written upon the subject. I know nothing of you personally, beyond the fact that you first visited South Africa as the agent of the Winchester Arms Co., and subsequently wrote letters for the New York WORLD. I know nothing about South Africa, of my own personal knowledge, and would be the last person to advise any one to leave comfortable homes and assured positions in this country in the hope of securing possible fortunes in so remote a locality as the Diamond Fields of South Africa. D. G. CROLY.

CONTENTS.

CHAPTER	PAGE
I. Description of the Diamond Country	11
II. Discovery of Diamonds	16
III. The Rush from the adjoining States	22
IV. Synopsis of my Diary on my First Visit	27
V. " " " "	31
VI. " " " "	36
VII. " " " "	40
VIII. Pniel and Klip Drift	44
IX. Other Mining Camps	50
X. Manner of Mining and Outfits Required, Finds, etc	58
XI. Discovery of the Dry Diggings and Visit to them	63
XII. Manner of Mining, my own Success, Finds, etc	67
XIII. Capetown	71
XIV. Port Elizabeth	77
XV. Ways to get to South Africa and the Mines from America	82
XVI. Delagoa Bay, Portuguese Settlement, and the Gold Mines	85
XVII. Large Diamonds of the World and other Information	89

ENGRAVINGS.

Map of South Africa (special.)
Capetown .... Frontispiece.
Diamond Washing 26
Dry Sifter 57
The House in which Diamonds were Found 63
Sketch of my own Claim at the Dry Diggings 68
Port Elizabeth 78

NOTES.

A SHILLING (1s.) is a little less than 25 cents in gold.

ONE POUND STERLING (£1) is a little less than $5; but for ordinary calculations it is best to consider 1s. as 25 cents, £1 as $5, and 10s. as $2.50.

OUTSPANNED means unyoked or unharnessed.

INSPAN means to harness up, or yoke the cattle.

DISTANCES are counted by hours—6 miles to an hour.

TREKING means moving on.

4 grains = 1 carat.

$151\frac{1}{4}$ carats = 1 ounce troy.

The exact weight *troy* is $3\frac{1}{4}$ grains = 1 carat.

THE SOUTH AFRICAN DIAMOND FIELDS.

CHAPTER I.

The diamondiferous regions of South Africa embrace an area of at least 10,000 square miles. They are situated between lat. 28° 30″ south, and long. 24° 28″ east (Greenwich). The Vaal River runs north and south through the center of this country, and most of the mining operations are carried on upon its borders. The Orange River runs along the southern part of the diamond district, and may be considered the southern boundary of the diamondiferous country, although a few diamonds have been found south of it in the Hopetown district of the colony. The Vaal River is a beautiful stream, lined nearly all its length with fine trees. The stream is 200 feet wide opposite the great camps, and for a mile it is deep and smooth water; above and below are rapids with a fall of about twenty feet, and then smooth, deep water again; it is like this all up and down the river, the stretches of smooth water hardly ever being more than a mile in length. During the months of June, July, and August the river becomes very low; but I have never heard of its becoming dry, as most of the South African rivers do during these months. There is plenty of grass for cattle—say a mile from the banks of the river. The climate of the diamond regions is similar to that of California, equable and extremely healthy. From March to September not a drop of rain falls. The nights during this period are quite cold; overcoats are in requisition from dawn to nine o'clock, and at night double blankets are required to insure a comfortable rest; ice would sometimes form one-quarter of an inch thick in the buckets left out at night with water in them. In September the warm weather sets in, accompanied by frequent thunder-storms. **A mild form of fever** is then prevalent (especially among those who do not take care of themselves), but very seldom proves fatal. Considering the number of people at the mines, and their manner of living in tents and wagons, and off badly-cooked food, and the poor sanitary measures enforced in camp, it is astonishing how healthy the people are.* Now that the British Government have taken charge, and sent an able magistrate (Mr. Campbell) to preside over the district, better sanitary measures will be enforced, and the healthiness of the camps will improve. After crossing the Orange River and entering the diamondiferous regions, the appearance of the country changes very perceptibly. Immense tracts or beds of water-worn pebbles of all colors are to be seen. The country is slightly undulating table-land, 5,000 feet above the level of the sea, with here and there a series of kopies (hills) that are covered with immense bowlders of iron stone. Water is scarce at certain seasons of the year. There are no rivers that contain water all the year round, excepting the Orange and Vaal. The farmers have to build dams at convenient places, which are filled during the rainy season, and the water lasts through the dry. At several of the inland farms where diamonds have been discovered, they have exhausted their supply of water by washing, and will have to cease mining until the rainy season sets in. Of course, this will be remedied by building larger dams. Most of the diamonds are found on the rand or spur of the kopies. The miners always look out for a "good wash" or deposit of water-worn pebbles. Diamonds are not found in all of these water-worn deposits, but they are never found where there are no water-worn pebbles. There are three different kinds of diamondiferous soil at Pniel. On our claim the first deposit, about six inches deep, was of a blackish color; the second, about five feet through, was of a reddish;

---

* CERTIFICATE.—I have much pleasure in availing myself of the present opportunity to certify, from personal experience, that in the latitude of the diamond fields, phthisis and ordinary pulmonary affections are of very rare occurrence. Patients whom we have sent there in the earlier stages of the above diseases are, to my own knowledge, in the enjoyment of re-established health, and in others—the despair of the physician—life has been prolonged for some years. The summer temperature is high, but does not enervate. The winter months are bright, clear, and bracing, affording a climate peculiarly adapted to patients troubled with disease of the lungs.

F. ENSOR, *Surgeon Port Elizabeth Provincial Hospital.*
PORT ELIZABETH, 23d *August*, 1870.

and the last, eight feet, of a whitish color—pebbles all the way down, showing that the whole deposit had been under the action of water. At most of the other camps the pay-dirt is not more than from six inches to three feet, while at Pniel it is sometimes twenty-five feet. Under these deposits there is a bed of yellowish clay, that hardens into rock as you go down. No other gravel deposit has yet been discovered under this rock, and, singular enough, no diamonds have been discovered in the ravines, even those which bound the richest kopies. It may be that the rains wash them to the river direct. The river has not been worked yet in a proper manner. Some tried to drag it, but never found any diamonds, because, in the first place, the diamond is bound to work its way to the very bottom among the interstices of rock; and in the second, the drags being flat, could not reach those deposits. The only way to get them out is to turn the river into a flume or canal, and pump out the holes. This will require capital, and I have no doubt will pay a rich dividend to any company that will undertake it. The diamond district is claimed by several white governments and native chiefs. That part which lies on the east bank of the Vaal River comprises part of the "Orange River Free State," a Dutch republic, settled by Dutch farmers who emigrated from the colony at its occupation by the English. Bloemfontien, a pretty place of about 1,000 inhabitants, is the capital. It is a well-laid out town, containing some very substantially-built and well-stocked stores, a first-class hotel, and several well-built churches. Here the President resides and the Legislature meets. The President is elected for a term of years. The present one (John Brand) is quite popular. He is very kind and genial to strangers. The English language is spoken as freely as the Dutch, and quite a number of Englishmen reside there. The Orange River Free State has just been recognized by the United States Government. Bloemfontien is about 100 miles from Pniel. There are about a dozen other towns within that distance of the mines situated in the Free State, Transvaal Republic, and "The colony." According to the Roman Dutch law, under which the constitution was formed, the State has no right over the minerals, excepting in Government lands; and when any of this land is sold, the purchaser has the right to the minerals. They may, however, alter this law, as far as the Government lands are concerned, and charge a royalty or tax of say 10s. a month to each miner who desires to work on Government lands. The diamondiferous land of the Free State which has as yet been discovered, is mostly owned by citizens who generally allow diggers to work on their land, and charge them about 10s. per month. These farms are generally from 6,000 to 18,000 acres in size, and can be purchased for from £5,000 to £10,000. Before diamonds were discovered upon them they could have been purchased for less than £2,000 each. The west bank of the Vaal River from the mouth of the Hart River is claimed by the Chief Jautjie, the Chief Waterboer, and the Transvaal Republic, another Dutch settlement of a later date than the Orange Free State. The capital of this republic is Pretoria, and the largest place is Potchefstrom, about 200 miles from and north of Pniel, a town of about 1,000 white inhabitants. The State is governed by a President and Legislature elected by the people; it has also been recognized by the United States Government. They are trying to get a sea-port at Ingack Island, Delagoa Bay, and will probably succeed. Now all their importations have to come through "The Colony," and pay colonial duty. Both the Free State and Transvaal Republic are anxious for American emigration, and large farms are offered to emigrants at a very low figure, and on time to emigrants who have means to stock them. The whole country consists of a vast undulating table-land, where anything can be raised if dams are built to supply water. The chief production of the country is wool. There are immense herds of sheep grazing from one end of the country to the other. Coffee, sugar, wheat, corn, and all kinds of fruit and vegetables, are raised to a certain extent; but as there are no rivers or railroads leading to the sea, it does not pay to raise these articles for export. In time, when the people or foreign capitalists can build a railroad, immense exports of the above productions will be made from these two republics.

From the mouth of the Hart River, on the west bank of the

Vaal, to the Orange River, and down to its mouth, the country is claimed by the Orange Free State and Jautjie. So far no license has been paid by the miners, and they have come to the conclusion that they never will pay any, unless forced to do so by the British Government, which has just stepped in and taken possession of the whole of the diamond district on both sides of the Vaal, and sent a magistrate there to look after things and stop the quarreling—a kind of way the British lion has of settling things. It may be best, after all, for the west bank diamond fields, as they were just on the point of declaring a republic of their own, which would have caused a bloody war, perhaps, of long duration, which would have effectually stopped diamond mining for the time being. A council was held a few months ago on the Klip Drift or west side, at which they decided that the Transvaal Republic owned that side of the river from the mouth of the Hart River. At this council there were present President Pretorius, of the Transvaal; President Brand, of the Free State; President Parker, who had been elected by the miners as President of the diamond district of the west side; Jautjie and Waterboer, two native chiefs who lived upon the land. At the decision of the council, the Transvaal Republic appointed a Mr. Owen as magistrate, and sent him to the great camp, Klip Drift, where he issued a proclamation and raised the Transvaal flag. The miners, not liking this arrangement, tore down the flag, and putting Mr. Owen into a boat, sent him across the river, and his tent after him, and refused to allow him to return. They also refused to recognize the Transvaal government authority over the diamond district, and they deposed Mr. Parker, and elected a Mr. Barker in his stead; they also elected twelve members for a council. Since then there has been constant quarreling going on until Mr. Campbell's arrival, when he stopped all further disputes by taking possession of and proclaiming the territory as British. I think the British Government will impose a slight tax only on miners, and at the same time allow them to work wherever they like, excepting on settled farms.

CHAPTER II.

During the year 1867, a trader was traveling in the Free State, and, stopping at a farm near the Vaal River, he observed a small boy playing with a peculiar-looking crystal. He carefully examined it, and remarked to the parents that he thought it was a diamond, and asked them what they would take for it. They laughed at the idea of its being a diamond, and told him he could have it for nothing. In passing through several towns on his way to the coast, he frequently showed it, and was laughed at when he mentioned that he thought it was a diamond. He became so disgusted that he was on the point of throwing it away, when he happened to show it to Dr. Atherstone, a scientific gentleman of Grahamstown, in the colony. Dr. A. was struck with its appearance, and immediately took its specific gravity, and, testing it in other ways, proved beyond doubt that it was a veritable diamond of 20 carats in weight. It was sent to Capetown, and there purchased by the Governor, Sir Philip Wodehouse, for £500. This affair created some excitement in the colony, but it soon died out.

About a year after this, a trader named Shalk Van Niekerk purchased the "Star of South Africa," a beautiful diamond of 83 carats, from a native doctor, in whose possession it had been for several years, and who had used it as a charm to cure diseases with among the natives. He said that he had found it on the north bank of the Orange River, about one hundred miles below the mouth of the Vaal. Van Niekerk gave him five hundred sheep for it, and taking it to Hopetown, sold it for £11,500 to the firm of Lilienfeld Brothers, who sent it to Europe, where it remained in the market in its rough state for some time, and no offer being made for it, the owners had it cut in Amsterdam, at their own risk. It turned out to be a beautiful first-water brilliant of 40 carats, and was purchased by the celebrated London firm of Hunt & Boskel. It is not generally known what price was paid for it; it is rumored from £6,500 to

£16,000. It is understood that H. & B. ask £25,000 for it now. The finding of the "Star of South Africa" caused great excitement in the colony, and a rush of traders took place immediately, who managed to purchase from the natives quite a lot of diamonds, among them the following: one of 47 carats was sent home by Messrs. Breda, Halket & Co., Capetown; a diamond of 30½ carats was found at Bloemhof, on the banks of the Vaal River; numerous other diamonds, of 5, 7, 12, 16, 20, 25, 30 and 40 carats were found during the next two years by natives, and all on the surface.

LIST OF DIAMONDS.

No. 1.—Found at the farm "De Kalk," division of Hopetown, by a child of Daniel Jacobs. Weight, 21 3-16th carats. Sold to the Government. The child had been in possession of the gem for some time, and she and some native children used it, with some other pretty stones, as a plaything. Mr. Schalk Niekerk, when on a visit one day to this place, was struck with the appearance of the stone. He got possession of it. It was afterward sent to Dr. Atherstone, in Grahamstown. The Doctor pronounced it to be a diamond of the first water. People, both natives and Europeans, then commenced to search.

No. 2.—Was found soon afterward by Mr. Duvenhage on his father's farm, "Paarde Kloof," along the Orange River, in the division of Hopetown. Weight, 8 13-16th carats. A beautiful stone, very regular in shape. Purchased by the Governor.

No. 3.—Found by a native along the Vaal River. Weight, 4 7-16th carats. Very eccentric shape, but very clear. Purchased by Mr. John Cruikshanks, who sent it to his father in Scotland.

No. 4.—Found by Mr. Hans Bezuidenhout, on Mr. Cloete's farm, "Mark's Drift," along the Orange River, division of Hopetown. Weight, 1½ carats, greenish color, defective in shape, and evidently broken. Presented to Mr. Chalmers by Mr. Bezuidenhout.

No. 5.—Found by Mr. Jacob Cloete, on a piece of Government ground along the Orange River, division of Hopetown. Weight, 3 4-16th carats, regular in shape and very brilliant. Has a very small black spot. Purchased by Mr. Lilienfeld, and sent by him to his friends in England.

No. 6.—Found by a Hottentot servant of Mr. Jan Duvenhage, on his master's farm, "Paarde Kloof" (same farm where No. 2 was found). Weight, 3 5-16th carats. Very regular in shape, and of first water. Purchased by the Governor.

No. 7.—Found by a Griqua near the Vaal River. Weight, 15¼ carats. Purchased from the Griqua by Mr. Radloff, and sold by Mr. Radloff to the Governor.

No. 8.—Found by a Griqua along the Vaal River, near Campbell, in

July, 1868. Weight, 12⅜ carats. Defective in shape, one end very much discolored and rather flat, the other end brilliant and like the point of a conical bullet. Purchased from the Griqua by Mr. Chapman, who has sent it home. This is the diamond found when Mr. Gregory was here.

No. 9.—Found by a Griqua in Waterboer's country, in August, 1868. Weight, 2 carats. First water. Regular shape. Purchased by Mr. Chapman.

No. 10.—Found by a Griqua near the junction of the Vaal and Riet Rivers, in September, 1868. Weight, 13 carats. Triangular shape. Color like polished steel. Purchased from the Griqua by Messrs. Wykeham & Co., and afterward sold by them to Mr. Maurice Joseph, of Capetown.

No. 11.—Found by a Bechuana beyond the Vaal River, in October, 1868. Weight, 9 carats. A very brilliant diamond, particularly well shaped. Purchased by the Governor.

No. 12.—Found by a native along the Vaal River, in October, 1868. Weight, 6 carats. Straw-colored. Defective in shape.

No. 13.—Found by a Bechuana along the Riet River, in October, 1868. Weight, 3 carats. Milky color. Has a small hole on one of the facets.

No. 14.—Brought in by a trader, who received it from a native beyond the Orange River, in October, 1868. Weight, 4 carats. Very regular in shape, and particularly sharp-pointed; very brilliant; has a small yellow spot on one of the facets, which gives the gem rather a yellow color.

No. 15.—Brought in by the same trader, in October, 1868. Weight, 1½ carats. (Nos. 14 and 15 were forwarded to Port Elizabeth, to be disposed of there.)

No. 16.—Found along the Vaal River, in November, 1868, by a native. Weight, about 2 carats. Defective in shape, and rather discolored. Purchased by Mr. Hond.

No. 17.—Found by a Bechuana beyond the Vaal River, in November, 1868. Weight, 4 carats. Very perfect in shape and very brilliant. This gem is still in the hands of the Hon. R. Southey, Colonial Secretary, and is still for disposal.

No. 18.—Found by Mr. David Bebell in the same locality where No. 11 was found. Weight, 9 carats. Very pure and very regular in shape, but it has a very large hole in it. Purchased by Mr. L. Lilienfeld. Found in December, 1868.

No. 19.—Found on the farm "Roode Kop," along the Orange River, in the division of Hopetown, in December, 1868. Weight, 1½ carats. Very inferior; discolored. Is now in possession of Mr. Lilienfeld.

No. 20.—Found by a Griqua along the Vaal River, and sold by him to Mr. Bebell, who sold it to Mr. Lilienfeld. Weight, 14 carats. Has several black spots, otherwise it would be a very brilliant stone.

Nos. 11 and 17 are the best diamonds that have yet been found; the most brilliant and regular in shape.

Other diamonds have been found besides these twenty, but I have only kept particulars of those which have passed through my hands. The foregoing information, therefore, can be depended upon.

W. B. CHALMERS, C. C. and R. M.

HOPETOWN, 20th January, 1869.

These natives would form themselves into long lines, joined hand in hand, and walk slowly over the ground and look for diamonds, especially after rain; and if they found one they would take it to a trader, and offer it to him at a most exorbitant price. If the trader were to make an offer he would never get the diamond, but by leaving the native to make the offer, he would gradually fall about 1,000 per cent. from his former demand. I have known a native ask £2,500 for a diamond that was finally purchased from him for £150, and that was paid in goods, and took three days to close the bargain. The natives will generally take blankets, beads, oxen, wagons, and sheep for their diamonds. They have been aware of the weight and water of diamonds, but not of their value. A company was formed in the colony who sent an agent up to the chief of the supposed diamond district, and obtained a concession of all the diamond fields on the west bank of the Vaal. They made no effort to find the deposits themselves, but put the whole district up for sale in Europe. This the company did not succeed in doing, and after the rush, finding that they could not hold the ground, they gave up the scheme as a bad job. The "Star of South Africa" was supposed to have been found on their possessions, and they tried through the colonial court to get possession of it, but failed in doing so, and had to pay costs besides.

It was not until 1870 that any one thought of organizing a prospecting company who would devote their time and energies to the exclusive hunting of the regular diamond deposits, and mining properly for them. King William's Town, a place of considerable importance in the colony, organized a prospecting company and sent it to the Vaal, under the superintendence of Mr. McIntosh. This company consisted of eight partners, four of whom furnished the money to outfit the expedition, and the other four were to do the prospecting and mining. At the same time, another similarly organized company started from Natal, under Captain Rolliston. These two parties met at Hebron, and were a little jealous of each other at first, but becoming better acquainted, this soon disappeared, and they commenced to prospect together on the west bank of the Vaal. Now, the natives were rather chary of letting white men prospect on their grounds. They seemed aware that, in case of the regular diamond deposit being discovered, a great rush would be made and their lands taken from them. So they would not allow these parties to touch the ground with pick or shovel. After prospecting, with sharp sticks only, for three months up and down the Vaal, at places where the natives had found diamonds on the surface, the two companies parted, Rolliston's remaining at Hebron, and McIntosh's following the west bank of the Vaal toward its mouth. They parted with the understanding that in case one party should discover a deposit, they should let the other know immediately, but secretly. It was a month after this that the McIntosh party were at Klip Drift, tired and disheartened, and thinking of giving it up, when a native was induced to inform them where he had found a diamond that he had in his possession. He took them half a mile from the drift or ford, to what is now known as the "Old Kopie," and pointed out the spot to them. They were not allowed to put a pick in the earth; but McIntosh, in turning over the soil at the roots of a thorn tree, discovered a half carat diamond. The party then determined to send for the Natal party, and to go to work on the kopie with pick and shovel, in spite of the natives. The kopie was about one thousand yards from the river bank; and upon the arrival of the Natal party they dug out a load, carted it down to the river, and washed it out with an Australian cradle, finding several diamonds therein. They must have lost a great many from the rudeness of their machinery. They worked on every day after this, in spite of the continued protests of the natives, and with uniform success. The diamondiferous soil lay in a triangular-shaped space about sixty yards in circumference, two sides bounded by a reef of amgdoline or pudding-stone, and the other by the plain. The rich soil was from six inches to three feet in depth. The latter were small basins or pockets. The McIntosh party worked up the left angle or reef, and the Natal party the right angle or reef. While piling up their "cascalho" one day, preparatory to hauling it to the river, a nine carat diamond made its appearance, which a native who was standing by immediately seized, and was making off with it when he was caught and compelled to give it up. He made a great disturbance about this, and complained to the chief, who, however, sustained the white men after hearing their story.

Now, these two parties had been working a month without letting any one know of their success, always asserting that they found no diamonds; but their constant labor had created suspicion, and several parties, mostly traders, hung around their camp watching them. One day, while Captain Rolliston was dumping a load of "cascalho" at the washing place, a five carat diamond rolled in sight of one of these outsiders, who immediately seized it and claimed it, in spite of Captain Rolliston having dug and hauled it to the river. He seized it on the grounds that as Captain Rolliston had said that they had found no diamonds, and he had found this one, he was consequently entitled to it; and Captain Rolliston had to prepare for a fight before he would give it up. This discovery caused great excitement, and all the traders immediately took up claims on the Old Kopie. In one month the McIntosh party took out 120 diamonds, valued at £6,000, the largest a beautiful thirty carat, another nine carat, and the balance from six carats down to a quarter of a carat. The Natal party took out 52 diamonds, valued at £40,000. They were mostly large-sized diamonds, among them a forty carat, valued at £9,000. Another party took out 50 diamonds, but I do not know the value of them. Other parties also did very well. There were 300 diamonds taken from this small triangle in less than two months, that were valued at over £80,000.

CHAPTER III.

About this time a trader, named Stafford Parker, became aware of these finds, and immediately wrote letters to that effect to different papers in the colony, but they were not believed. At last a young man, named Slater, wrote a letter to his father at Port Elizabeth, confirming Parker's statements, and urging his friends to come to the fields immediately. The consequence was, that a rush was made from all parts of the "Colony," "Free State," and "Transvaal Republic." Every paper from every town and village was teeming with the names of people who had gone and were going to the diamond fields, in all conceivable kinds of conveyances. Some went with Scotch carts drawn by four oxen, and laden with cradles, provisions, and mining tools, and the owners walking (in some cases) 500 miles. Some started without any outfit or conveyance whatever, and tramped over 600 miles, sleeping in the Veldt, with the broad canopy of heaven for their shelter, begging their food from the wayside farms, and in one case arriving at the diamond fields, and making a fortune in a week. A Dutch boer (farmer) would leave his farm in the care of the servants, inspanned sixteen oxen to his ponderous African wagon, put his vrow, kinders, a few household gods and provisions into it, not forgetting an immense supply of coffee (without which no South African boer ever travels), and treked to the diamond fields, imagining that he and his family would spend a few weeks pic-nicking, and employ their leisure hours picking up diamonds by the handsful, and return home and lay in a fresh supply of coffee. In some instances, they were rewarded with a fortune; in a great many other instances, finding that diamond mining meant hard labor from early morn "till dewy eve;" and no Dutchman likes hard labor. They meandered round for a few days, looking at the hard workers with amazement, became disgusted with Englishmen who would work, resolved not to disgrace themselves by doing likewise for any amount of money, and returned home, vrow, kinders, household gods and all, and resumed their pipes and coffee, wiser, but I cannot say better men. Now, I don't mean to say all Dutchmen are like that, but the majority are. I have known some who have brought their families to the mines, and a few servants, and have worked as hard as any Englishman; one family, in particular, Waldecks, from the "Free State," that made a fortune at Pniel. He and his servants would do the digging and washing, and his wife and children would sort out the washed gravel, and pick out the diamonds.

All kinds of people went to the mines; among them British officers, stationed in the colony, who had never handled anything heavier than a sword on parade day, obtained leave of absence for a few months, went to the mines, and worked like navvies, and, in several cases, made fortunes. Merchants, clerks, mechanics, laborers, and chronic loafers even, could not resist the fascination of diamond digging. Some, though, worked for months, and never found a single diamond, having a twenty foot claim surrounded by four other twenty foot claims, every one of which was rich in the gems but his own. On my way to the diamond fields, I have met Dutchmen returning from there, who swore that it was all a humbug, and that there were no diamonds to be found, when an hour before, I had met a fortunate individual who had shown me a dozen diamonds that he had dug out himself, and who, in the first flush of fortune, was rushing home to spend it, and return again to the fields, where, perhaps, he would be doomed to disappointment.

Most of the diggers went direct to Klip Drift and the Old Kopie, taking up claims adjacent to the celebrated triangle. This kopie was soon all taken, and then further arrivals tried the next kopie down the river, called the Second, or Town Kopie. This was soon taken up in claims, and then the next arrivals moved farther down the river to the Third, or Colesburg Kopie, called so on account of a Colesburg party discovering diamonds upon it. These three kopies, or hills, are about two miles long from the Drift where the wagons ford the river to the bottom of the Colesburg Kopie. No diamonds were found immediately below this last kopie. The river front of these kopies is deep and still water, having rapids above and below. The river was crossed by yawl boats opposite the great camp, half a dozen of which were running, and charging 6*d.* a passenger. These two miles of kopies were called Klip Drift, or Rocky Ford, from the name of the ford that the miners crossed the Vaal by. The chief camp was pitched on the Second, or Middle Kopie, between the river and the mines, the latter generally being about 500 yards from the river, and on the top of the kopies that had an average elevation of 100 feet above the river. The tops of these kopies were flat, and covered with a deposit of water-worn gravel or pebbles—often by large bowlders and rough rocks, that had to be removed with a crowbar. No houses were built at this time, the miners living in tents and wagons only.

A kind of provisional government was now instituted for the purpose of keeping order in the camp. The miners held a meeting, and elected four members of council and a president. Stafford Parker was elected president; rules and regulations were drawn up, and all newcomers were compelled to sign them, as well as those who had been there from the first. There were two sets: one for mining, and the other for defense. These rules are given in another page.

Immediately opposite the Town Kopie, on the Free State side, and on the Pniel mission estate, a Dutchman, who had encamped temporarily, found a half carat diamond on the surface, close to his wagon. This side of the Vaal, for fifteen miles up and down the river, is owned by the Berlin missionary station, called Pniel, some three miles up the river, under the charge of the Rev. Mr. Kallenburg. The Dutchman reported this find to Mr. Kallenburg, and requested permission to mine there. This was granted, with the proviso that a quarter of the value of all finds should be handed over to Mr. K. After a while, other Dutchmen, getting wind of this, obtained permission also. The missionary would only let those with whom he was acquainted, or who were well vouched for, mine on the estate; but in less than a month, he had 300 families, mostly Dutch, working opposite the great camp. He derived a revenue of at least £1,000 per month.

A great many new arrivals, and parties from the Klip Drift side, applied for permission to mine on the estate, and were refused; but the missionary, finding that parties were coming over in the night—cradles, tools, and all—and taking up claims, working anyhow, and not paying one-quarter of the finds either, called a council of Berlin missionaries, who concluded to let any one who could get a voucher from Stafford Parker, President of the Vigilance Committee of Klip Drift, mine on the estate. The consequence was, a rush from the Klip Drift side of at least 500 men, who soon took up every available claim. The missionaries appointed a committee to look after their interests. They drafted the following rules:

"That all applicants should sign before being allowed to mine on the estate.

"A claim should consist of thirty feet square (to be given out by one of the committee) for each cradle.

"Whenever a diamond is found by a miner, it must be reported at the committee tent within twenty-four hours. These to be weighed.

"If the miner sells the diamond, he must pay the missionaries' agent one-quarter of the proceeds. If he does not sell it, the committee will appraise it, and the miner pay as above."

The above are the most important resolutions. There were several others of minor importance. It was soon found out that not one-half of the miners reported their finds, and that there was a great anxiety for a reduction of the tax; so at another meeting it was resolved to impose a tax of 10s. a month on every washing machine, and take off the one quarter tax on the finds. This gave better satisfaction to the miners, and a sure income to the society. At present there must be over 1,000 cradles at work on the Pniel estate, yielding the missionary society a revenue of £2,500 a month. As in other mineral countries, new places, a few miles off, were discovered, and rushes from both camps made to them. These places generally proved to be of small extent, and those parties which first arrived took up all the good claims, while hundreds returned to their old camp disappointed, and probably finding the claim they had deserted had been taken by a newcomer. Still a great many remained at such places as Gong Gong, Good Hope, Bad Hope, Lucas Kopie, Webster's Kopie, and Sifonel, which places extended some twenty miles down the river and up the river, as far as Hebron. New places are still being constantly found, and the "cascalho" deposits extend on a very large extent of country.

DIAMOND WASHING.

CHAPTER IV.

I WILL now give a synopsis of my own diary to show a miner's every-day life, traveling and mining.

Business had called me to Colesburg, a frontier town of the colony; and, as I had a few months to spare, I concluded to devote it to diamond mining, and give it a practical trial, as I had been in California, and had done all kinds of gold mining and working. I invented a machine for diamond washing, somewhat similar to a longtom and cradle combined, which, after a trial at the mines, and a few alterations, proved to be quite a success. I had this machine made at Colesburg, put together with screws, and taken apart for easy transport. There is an engraving of it on page 26.

COLESBURG, *June* 29*th*, 1870.—Everything ready to start for the diamond fields, 170 miles in a N. W. direction. There are three partners in the concern: Messrs. Rawstorne, Plewman, and myself. Messrs. R. and P. are merchants at Colesburg. We take two colored boys with us. We have sent on a Scotch cart, drawn by four oxen, in charge of two other boys. This cart contains our washing machine, pump, hose, and mining tools. We expect to come up with them about half way to the fields.

Rawstorne and I travel in a six-mule spring wagon, which will also contain our provisions, carpenter's tools, bedding and clothing; we have very few of the latter, but they are substantial. We believe in traveling light, and leaving our "store" clothes at home. We hired the wagon and mules for three months. The balance of our outfit, including the Scotch cart and four oxen, cost us £100. Plewman remains in Colesburg to settle some business, and then follows in his own trap.

30TH.—Some of the citizens of Colesburg gave us a dinner in honor of our being the Colesburg pioneers to the diamond fields. James Hennessy's and Mad. Cliquot's names were frequently heard at the table, and they were passed round till some of the party couldn't rest. We managed to escape at 3 P.M., and started off in fine style, with three cheers from our late hosts, and accompanied by several carriage loads of ladies and gentlemen for some miles on the road. Outspanned (unhitched) for the night at a farm nine miles from Colesburg, and slept for the first time in our wagon.

July 1st.—Arose at daylight; had coffee, inspanned, or hitched up, and made the Orange River Drift at Rosse's Ferry. As the river was too high to cross the drift, we crossed on the ferry, and entered the Orange River Free State, a young Republic. Twenty years ago, if a traveler arrived in London, who had crossed the Orange River of South Africa, he was lionized, and made an honorary member of the Traveler's Club. It is becoming common in these days, and the Zambesi, 1,000 miles further north, is now the line of interest. At 2 P.M., we arrived at Phillapolis, a village of 500 inhabitants, most of whom had gone, or were preparing to go to the diamond fields. We hear very encouraging news here. After dinner we treked (moved on), passing through an immense swarm of locusts, which come up against your face with a thump that startles you. We made twelve miles farther, and outspanned for the night.

2d.—Inspanned at daylight again, and made ten miles; had breakfast, and made Fauresmith, a town of about 1,000 inhabitants, at 3 P.M. Outspanned and had dinner just upon the outskirts of the town. A large number of the inhabitants had gone to the diamond fields. All the carpenters' shops were busy making cradles for washing the "cascalho." Made twelve miles more, and camped at Schietmakaar for the night. Since we have crossed the Orange River, the appearance of the country has changed; we now see immense tracts of slightly undulating and gravelly ground between ridges of bowlder-crowned kopies or hills. We are now 5,000 feet above the level of the sea. The climate is delightful; cold enough at night to require blankets, and just warm enough during the day to dispense with coats. No rain at this season of the year. The farmers build dams at convenient places on their farms (generally on the side of a rise), in which water enough is caught from the winter storms to last through the dry season. We had to pay 1s. at some farms to be allowed to water our stock at the dams.

3d.—Made a farm at 9 A.M., ten miles from where we were last night. This farm is situated on the Reit River. Saw a large number of bucks (springbok), but could not get within range, as we had no riding-horse, and the ground was not rugged enough to stalk them. At 8 P.M., having followed the Reit River, we crossed it, and outspanned; found our cart and its contents, and another ox wagon of diamond seekers.

4th.—Arrived at 10 A.M. at Jacobsdahl, the last town on the route to the diamond fields, and about forty miles from them. This place has about 500 inhabitants. There are several large stores here; one kept by Isaac Sonnenberg, who has lived a great deal in America; he has a fine stock of provisions and mining tools. To-day, being the anniversary of American Independence, we celebrated it by firing a salute of sixteen shots in ten seconds from a "Winchester Repeater," which gathered the Dutch around us in swarms. We then spent an hour sampling champagne. Inspanned and treked. Before leaving, Mr. Sonnenberg showed me four diamonds, one of twenty-six carats, and three of one carat each; he values the twenty-six carat one at £2,000. After crossing the Modder River, we made Du Forts Farm, and outspanned for the night. Diamonds have been picked up on the surface at this farm. The family will not, however, allow any one to work on it yet, chiefly on account of the scarcity of water.

5th.—Arrived at Pniel Mission Station at 12 noon. Hearing that the mining on this side of the river is rather better than that on the other side, we asked permission of Mr. Kallenburgh, the missionary, to mine on the estate. He declined to grant it till after a contemplated meeting of the Berlin missionaries in the Free State, which would take place next month. We then went to Klip Drift, three miles further down the river; outspanned on an island in the middle of the Drift, and while the boys were cooking dinner, took a walk down the Pniel side of the river, where we found about fifty men, women, and children working—the men digging and washing the women and children sorting the washed pebbles. The scene was intensely exciting, and we wanted to pitch in immediately, and take a claim. We were shown diamonds right and left, and observed with what ease a diamond could be distinguished from the pebbles from which it is taken. The mining was carried on within fifty yards of the river, on the top of a rand or spur of a large kopie. This spur runs down the river, and parallel with it. After digging out the soil, it is carted down, and dumped on the bank, washed in a cradle, and emptied on a table; where the sorters sit all day picking out the precious gems. The sensation of picking out a diamond must be exquisite to the finder, if it has such an effect as it had on me when, looking on, I saw one found. The scene is very picturesque and refreshing to us who have not seen a tree or (excepting the Orange and Modder) a river with water in it since we left Colesburg. The great camp of Klip Drift is just opposite, and the hills are covered with miners, and the banks of the river with washers. The scene is so intensely exciting to us, we want to begin at once, and feel as if we can hardly wait till morning. I wonder what my dreams will be about to-night; nothing but diamonds, diamonds, diamonds, I expect, and some very extensive ones, too, no doubt. Met Mr. Green, late civil commissioner of Colesburg, who has obtained permission from Mr. Kallenburg to mine on the estate. He has two very large claims, and he showed us five diamonds that he had already taken out, ranging from $\frac{1}{2}$ to $5\frac{1}{2}$ carats. The soil is of a reddish color, and the miners only go down about six inches or a foot. (Since the above date they have gone down over twenty feet, finding diamonds all the way). The miners are chiefly Dutch; very few Englishmen. On this side they are encamped under the trees between their mine and washing place. While we were looking on, a Dutchman found a $15\frac{1}{2}$ carat diamond, worth £1,000, while digging, and without washing; he yelled out and howled around there like a crazy man, and everybody left their work, and made a rush to see it. He won't sleep any to-night. I expect he'll invest in a bag of coffee to-morrow. Returning to our wagon, we had an excited dinner, with our eyes opened as big as saucers, looking between every bite for diamonds in the river sand. I see that I am bound to get round-shouldered if I remain at the mines long. Every fellow you meet is looking down, as if he had stolen something from you. He is only looking for diamonds. He wears out the toes of his boots in an incredibly short space of time, kicking over all the stones he comes across as he goes from his mine to his washing or meals. When we arrived at headquarters at Klip Drift (the water at the ford was up to our wagon bed, and quite swift), we met Meader's party from Philipstown, near Colesburg. (They are friends of Rawstorne's). They had found an eighteen carat diamond the day before, and Morritz Unger, the diamond merchant, who has just arrived from Europe, offered them £550 for it, but they refused, and one of the party took it to Bloemfontien, where he expects to get £600 for it. I saw Mr. Unger purchase two diamonds to-day; one was $6\frac{5}{16}$, and the other $5\frac{5}{16}$ carats; he paid £165 for them.

CHAPTER V.

JULY 6TH.—Went to the top of the Colesburg or third kopie, and took a claim of twenty feet square, being fortunate in finding one just in the middle of the crowd, which seemed to have been overlooked, and around all sides of which diamonds had been found. We then took two more claims upon the outskirts of the hill, and put up beacons on them. There are about fifty claims taken up on this kopie. We went to the river and found a place for our cradle about 500 yards below our mines. We then inspanned and treked to the washing place, where we pitched our tent. After luncheon we went to work with axe, pick and shovel, and cleared and cut a place for our cradle and "cascalho." The underbrush was very thick. We set our sorting-table under the shade of a large willow tree. At night our hands were full of blisters and thorns. Went up to headquarters, where we signed the rules, mining and defensive, paying 2s. 6d. for each privilege. This tax is imposed for the purpose of keeping the drift in good order, and paying the expenses of the committee. The miners are a peaceable body of men, a little gambling and drinking going on, and once in a while a fist fight; but no shooting or cutting has occurred as yet. Called upon Mr. Unger, the diamond merchant, who came out from England at the same time that I did. He showed me more than one hundred diamonds that he had purchased. He had just sealed up a larger quantity that he was sending to Port Elizabeth and Europe. He will leave soon for Colesburg to get more money, having spent £10,000 in diamonds in less than a month. He tells me that this is the richest diamond country in the world, and that he has seen some immense ones since his arrival. He says that about twenty-five diamonds a day are being found on each side of the river. The majority of diamonds on this side are large, from five to forty carats; but on the other side they are smaller, but more plentiful on each claim. There are some parties on this side who have been working for weeks and have not found a single diamond; but they are sticking to it, and will, no doubt, eventually be rewarded.

7TH.—At sunrise we had coffee, and went up to the claims and marked off the boundary with large stones, increasing the blisters on our hands. Breakfast at 9 A.M. As we were expecting our cart, we went up to meet it. Stopped at Atwell's store, a large tent containing an extensive stock of goods; purchased six feet of one-inch lumber, at 1s. per foot; also some butter at 2s. 6d. per lb. Met Mr. King, a member of the Colonial Parliament, who had just arrived. He had picked up a sack of potatoes that we had dropped on the road some miles back; he divided it with us. Returned to camp without seeing the cart. Invented and made a dry sifter to use at the mine. This sieve has been extensively copied at the mines, and hundreds are to be seen there; it has been christened by the miners the "Yankee Baby." Meader picked up two more diamonds to-day out of his claim, worth about £70. A Dutchman picked up a seven and a half carat diamond from his claim next to ours; it is worth £120. Met Messrs. Dees and Lamb, of Natal. Lamb is a member of Rolliston's party, who made such a rich haul from the old kopie.

8th.—At daylight went to the claim and dug a hole two feet deep and three by six feet in width and breadth. Struck the bed rock. Weather so cold that we had to work with our gloves and pea-jackets on until we got warmed up. The soil is reddish, and full of round water-worn pebbles of all colors, some very pretty, such as I have seen in cheap jewelry at home. We dug out and sifted several loads of " cascalho." Saw our cart coming over the hill and conducted it to camp. After breakfast we unloaded it, and fixed up our " Tom " and pump for washing next day. Went up to headquarters. Meader had picked up a four carat diamond to-day; it was only worth about £40, on account of there being two black spots in it. His claim is on the second kopie. A two carat diamond was found next to our claim to-day.

9th.—At daylight we took two of our boys and dug out five loads of " cascalho," and then went to another of our claims and dug out two cart loads to secure it. The mining law requires that a claim must be worked at least every three days. Each partner is entitled to a twenty-foot claim, and we have taken three at different localities. We then hauled two cart-loads of sifted " cascalho " to our washing place, and commenced our first washing. Found that our pump would not throw enough water, and consequently the " Tom " principle was a failure. So we altered it into a cradle by cutting off the lower part and putting rockers on it. We put the dirt in at the top of the twelve-foot sluice, and let the water wash it down into the rocker. By this time it is quite loosened, and passes through the different sieves quickly with the assistance of a little rocking. We had to take out the perforated zinc and replace it with wire, as there were not sufficient holes in the zinc, consequently it soon choked up. The upper sieve has half-inch holes, sheet iron; the middle sieve is one eighth of an inch, wire mesh; the bottom is one sixteenth, wire mesh. No stone of any value will pass through this. Several more diamonds found near our claim to-day.

10th, Sunday.—All mining ceased to-day. All the stores and saloons are closed, and Divine service is being held in the committee tent. The Rev. Mr. Wills, of the Church of England (from Potchefstrom, Transvaal Republic), officiating. It was well attended. After the service, the mail arrived from Jacobsdahl and the Colony. It was brought from Jacobsdahl by private hands, and a sixpence extra was charged on each letter, and two pence on each newspaper. The mail left at 2 P.M. for Jacobsdahl, so as to arrive in time to catch the colonial post. I met Mr. McIntosh, of the King William's Town party. He showed me a box of ninety odd diamonds, ranging from half a carat to thirty carats in size. The thirty carat one is first water, and nearly round. A nine carat diamond in the lot is a perfect octohedron, and of the first water. He says that the thirty carat is worth £3,500, and the nine carat one about £300. The whole lot is valued at £6,000. Spent the afternoon in wandering around the kopies and river bank, examining the mines and washing machines. Of the latter there are a great variety, some being made of old gin cases set on rockers. Had a square meal to-day.

11TH.—Hauled down six cart loads of dirt to-day, and washed out part of it. *Nary diamond.* A few were taken out of our kopie to-day by our neighbor. Twenty-five diamonds were taken out of the claims on the Pniel side to-day, just opposite to us.

12TH.—Mr. Plewman having arrived, he and I went on a prospecting trip for a new claim, leaving Rawstorne and the boys to try their luck at the old claims. We went to the rear of the old kopie, to a native kraal, or village, and Mr. Plewman persuaded one of the natives to show us some spot where diamonds had been found on the surface by his tribe. He volunteered to do so if we would give him 1s., which we did, and he took us about half a mile further inland, and showing us a gravelly spot, said that a great many diamonds had been picked up there; so we beaconed off a claim and returned to camp, where we found that Rawstorne had washed out four loads without success. *No diamonds.* A twenty-six carat diamond was found on the second kopie to-day. Quite a large addition to the population during the last week.

13TH.—Rawstorne and two of the boys went over to our

new claim; it is two miles off. Dug out and hauled down two loads to the river; washed it out, but found *no diamonds*. We then washed out two loads from our first claim, and found ONE DIAMOND worth £8. We then all took a drink and had a square meal served up. A thirteen carat diamond was found on our kopie to-day, and a sixteen carat one on the second kopie, besides several small ones. Twenty-five diamonds found on the Pniel side to-day. Dr. Shaw, a guest of ours, and a geologist, from Colesburg, who is here taking notes, informed me that the Dutch are selling their diamonds very cheap on the Pniel side; so I gave him £20 to invest in small diamonds for me.

14TH.—Met Mr. Marshal, of Natal gold notoriety. He has just arrived with a large party who left Natal a month ago. They came in ox wagons 450 miles. While washing to-day, Mr. Hamilton, a photographer from Craddock, in the Colony, came down with his apparatus and took a picture of our party, machines, niggers, and all. We ordered a lot of them. He has just taken a panoramic view of both sides of the river. A Mr. Proctor found a twenty-nine carat diamond to-day on the second kopie; it is worth £2,000. They are still finding a number of small ones on the Pniel side.

15TH.—Washing and mining all day. *No diamonds*. A Dutchman named Waldeck took out a seventeen carat diamond to-day from his claim on the Pniel side. It is of a yellowish color. He asks £800 for it. Mr. Proctor took out another diamond to-day from the second kopie; it weighs five carats. Dr. Shaw purchased a beautiful half-carat diamond for me to-day for £3. Unger says he will try and get me a claim from the missionary (on the Pniel side), who is a countryman of his.

CHAPTER VI.

JULY 16TH.—Great excitement at headquarters to-day. Two young men who have lately arrived from London, named Webb and Pasno, the latter the son of a London diamond merchant, have just arrived from the Transvaal Republic, where they had obtained a concession of the diamond fields for thirty years from the President of that Republic, who claims this part of the country as belonging to the Transvaal. These young men have come down to inform the miners that they will be charged a tax of 10s. a month for the privilege of mining. The consequence is, that a meeting has been called by the President of the Council, Stafford Parker. About 500 miners responded. The President communicated the above intelligence to them, and asked them what they intended to do? They replied that "they were not going to pay one penny to any one for the privilege of mining; that they were not going to recognize the authority of the Transvaal Republic over the mines; and that, if Messrs. Pasno and Webb did not sign the rules, and recognize the president and council of the mines, they would put them through the river." Messrs. Pasno and Webb signed the rules. At the close of the meeting, a deputation of citizens from the Transvaal read a protest, signed by a large number of citizens of the Transvaal, against their President conceding the ground to any company whatever.

17TH.—Dr. Shaw purchased six diamonds for me at Pniel. One of the McIntosh party took me to the old kopie, and gave me the history of the first diamond discovery, and the working of the celebrated triangle (as described in Chapter II.)

19TH.—Mr. Plewman has just returned from Hebron, twenty miles up the river. There he met a Mr. Robinson, a trader, who showed him ninety diamonds, chiefly large ones (one of forty carats), that he had purchased from the natives, who had picked them up from the surface in that neighborhood. There are about 100 miners working there now.

20TH.—A 69½ carat diamond was found to-day next to Proctor's claim, on the second kopie. It is a miserable specimen, fit for nothing but boart. They ask £400 for it; it will not fetch more than £100 in Europe. Since writing the above, I learn that this diamond is an old stager that has been to Capetown, and sent back here for a soft purchaser. Fifteen diamonds have been picked up near Proctor's claim within the last three days. Another seventeen carat diamond found on the Pniel side to-day.

21ST.—Captain Gordon, late of Her Majesty's Army, found three diamonds to-day at his claim at Pniel; one is a beauty of two carats.

22D.—Dug down into the bed of a ravine that takes off the *debris* of the old kopie, just under the rich triangle. The bed rock or clay was soon reached, but the farther we went into this yellow clay the harder it became, until at three feet it was hard as rock. We hauled several loads of it to our washing place, and after puddling the clay, succeeded in washing it, but found no diamonds. Now, the washing from this rich triangle must have passed into this ravine, but still no diamonds have ever been found in it. The only way in which I can account for it is, that the deposit must have been but recently uncovered, and no diamonds have been washed from it by nature; or the rains, being so very heavy, have carried the diamonds that may have been washed out clear through the ravine to the Vaal River, about 1,000 yards distant.

23D.—A miner found seven diamonds in his claim at Pniel to-day. They are digging much deeper there now. Some have gone four feet, finding a good wash all the way, while on this side the general run is six inches or a foot only. I purchased a beautiful octohedron diamond to-day, weighing $1\frac{5}{10}$ carat, for £8.

24TH.—The President issued an order or command for all the miners to arm themselves, and assemble at headquarters at noon. About 800 of us met, armed with all kinds of guns. We learned that at Hebron a Dutchman had shot a native in the leg, who had stolen something from him, and was running away. The native chief and some of his men had captured the Dutchman, given him an awful beating, and robbed him of £75 worth of goods. The President told us we were called together to volunteer and arrest the chief and his associates in the affair, and also the Dutchman, and fetch them to the council for a proper trial; for it was not policy to allow the natives to arrest and punish any white man in the mines. Two hundred volunteers were called for who had horses. These immediately responded; and under command of McIntosh, started for Jautjie's kraal down the river, where the Dutchman was supposed to have been taken.

25TH.—The volunteers found the Dutchman was at Hebron; so they rode over there, and found him in the hands of Jautjie's son. They arrested the whole batch of them; and after a little resistance, brought them into camp, where they were kept under guard in the committee tent. They will be tried to-morrow by the committee or council. About 100 men were allowed to go over by the missionary society to the Pniel side. As we had only found one diamond on this side of the river, though constantly working, Rawstorne went over and secured a claim of twenty feet square, near to where diamonds are being found every day. He purchased a small cradle for £2 10s., and he and two of the boys went to work, while I and the other boys run the machine on this side. We also set up a young man named Bowler in a claim on the second kopie; we to furnish him with a boy, provisions, and tools, and wash his " cascalho," and he to give us half of the proceeds of his finds.

26TH.—As we have found no diamonds on this side for two weeks, we have concluded to move everything to the Pniel side, and put the whole of our force to work at that claim, and give up those on this side. We have seven boys now that we give a shilling a day to, and find in food. One attends to the cattle, one cooks, and the other five mine and wash, while R. and I sort at the tables. R. and I signed the rules at Pniel this morning, among which the most important one is, that we must report our finds to the committee within twenty-four hours; they will weigh them, and, after we sell them, we must pay them one-fourth of the proceeds.

27TH.—The trial of the prisoners broke up in a row yesterday, and the miners elected twelve new committee men, and had a fresh trial, which resulted in making Jaäijie refund the £75 worth of goods, and the Dutchman was fined £25 for shooting the Kaffir. Captain Gordon found an imperfect $7\frac{3}{4}$ carat diamond to-day, worth £50.

28TH.—I purchased a bright yellow diamond to-day, weighing $2\frac{1}{16}$ carat, for £20. I also purchased some boart, at 30s. a carat. I also made arrangements to purchase a farm of 30,000 acres, fronting on the Vaal River, between this and Hebron, for an American Company. If it is worked on a large scale it will pay immense dividends, if anything like the Pniel estate in richness. About fifty diamonds a day are now being found at the diggings, some large and some small.

30TH.—An $8\frac{2}{3}$ carat diamond found to-day next to our claim. "Nary diamond" have we found since the 13th. A gentleman took me on one side to-day, and informed me that, as he saw that I was going deep in the mine, and that as he knew I should find diamonds at a great depth, he would let me into a secret, and that was, that at a depth of ten feet, he had found more diamonds than nearer the surface; and, as all the miners were under the impression that there were none below a depth of four feet, he suggested that we should keep it a secret until the miners had worked their claims out to this depth and left them, and then that we should make a contract for the whole kopie, and work it out to the bed rock with a large force of natives. I told him I would think about it. (The miners found it out themselves shortly afterward).

AUGUST 1ST.—Rawstorne found two diamonds to-day out of the claim on the Pniel side after washing out four loads. Our claim is about fifty yards from the washing place. We moved our large cradle over and set it up. It works much better now, and with the force we have we can manage to wash and sort fifteen loads a day. At daylight we go to the mine, and by 9 o'clock we have dug out and sifted fifteen loads of "cascalho," hauling it down to the river in the meanwhile. At 9 o'clock we breakfast, and then, while the boys wash, we sort. At 1 P.M. we have luncheon, and then resume our washing and sorting till 6 P.M.; then we have dinner. On moonlight nights some of the miners dig and sift till 10 o'clock.

CHAPTER VII.

August 3.—The President of the Transvaal Republic, Mr. Pretorius, and the President of Klip Drift Diamond Fields, Mr. Parker, called upon me to-day and examined my machines for washing and sifting. The former has taken up a claim on the Klip Drift side, and works at it himself like a navvy. He is on a visit to the fields for the purpose of proving the claim of the Transvaal Republic to them. A conference is to be held next week five miles up the river, on the Klip Drift side, at which the Presidents of the Transvaal Republic, Orange Free State, Diamond Fields, and three native chiefs, who all laid claim to the territory on the west bank of the Vaal River, from the mouth of the Hart River, running north, will be present. A man named Jacobs found a $43\frac{1}{4}$ carat diamond to-day, valued at £1,000.

4th.—Diamonds are being constantly found all around us. We are sinking very deep in our claim in comparison to our neighbors. It will take us three months to work out our claim. The running expenses of our party of two white men, seven Kaffirs, and Bowler is about £40 a month.

8th.—The miners made arrangements for a subscription ball in honor of President Pretorius. It was successfully arranged, and was held in President Parker's tent. There were about one hundred and fifty gentlemen, in all conceivable costumes, from the swallow-tail to a clean mining suit. Sixteen ladies graced the ball with their presence. There was no roof to the tent; the floor was washed gravel from the mines. A few tallow candles dimly illuminated this gay and festive scene, and the moon had to do the balance. At one end a table was set with bottles of James Hennessy, wine, and soda water, which were kept continually in motion. The reserve stock of liquors and a lot of pies and cakes were lying near the side of the tent behind the bar, and a number of individuals reached under and cribbed a quantity, passing them round among the outsiders. The music consisted of an accordeon, fiddle, flute and bass drum. Although we did not have all we could wish for, our ball passed off pleasantly. We meandered to work again at daylight.

10TH.—Our bottom sieve being worn through, we had great difficulty in procuring another. We had to pay 15s. for a piece two feet square, ordinarily worth 1s. per foot.

11TH.—Purchased a lot of diamonds to-day, among them a most beautiful half carat octohedron, from a person who found it near our claim. It looks as if it had been cut. I had it set in a ring by a jeweler who has opened a shop at the mines.

13TH.—Washed out seven loads, and found *one* diamond. After dinner went over to Klip Drift to see the new billiard saloon of Sangers, of Bloemfontein It is a frame, covered with canvas on the sides and an iron roof. Sanger has been taking £60 a day since he opened. Black pool seems to be the ruling game. About twelve or fifteen men are playing all day and night, at 1s. each every half hour, and during that time they never take less than two drinks. Then there are about four card parties kept going day and night at unlimited loo.

14TH.—Met Sonnenburg, of Jacobsdahl, who informs me that he has secured four large farms on the Vaal River, below Pniel. Diamonds have been found on the surface of all of them by the natives. Sonnenburg intends to raise a stock company, and mine the farms on a large scale, and also turn the river on their fronts and work the bed of it.

15TH.—Wesser found a sixteen carat diamond to-day on this side.

16TH.—Our party found a half-carat diamond.

17TH.—We have now gone down ten feet; the soil has changed to a whitish color, but still contains a great number of water-worn pebbles.

18TH.—Met Mr. Farseneau, Portuguese Consul at Potchefstrom, Transvaal. He is also in the mercantile line at Potchefstrom, and is anxious that Americans should come to the Transvaal with capital and develop the country. He says there is an immense field for legitimate speculation in that country. A thirty-six carat diamond was found by Webster at a kopie three miles below here. A twenty-six carat one was found on the Colesburg Kopie.

19TH.—Our party found a one carat diamond, triangular shaped. As a rush was being made to Webster's Kopie, Rawstorne went down there and took up a claim. He managed to get one on the outskirts of the kopie; worked it all day, but could find no wash or "cascalho."

22D.—We found a 1¾ carat diamond. R. returned in disgust from Webster Kopie with the two boys, not having found any indication of diamonds in his claim. Our Koranna, named Hendrik, stole a diamond from our lower sieve, and tried to sell it to a friend of ours, who took it from him and gave it to us. We questioned Hendrik about it. He said he had found it on the Klip Drift side while walking along. As this was the second affair of the kind from him, I felt certain he had stolen it, and I complained to the committee. They said they could not punish him unless it was proved that he had stolen it. So I returned and told Hendrik, in a mild and kind tone, that if ever I caught him stealing a diamond from our party, I would blow his brains out. He reformed!

24TH.—Mr. De Kock, from Hopetown, informed me last night that he had worked in the fields for three months, and was £120 out. He was becoming discouraged, and would soon leave; he looked very blue. At noon to-day I met him tearing down the road, with a countenance as radiant as an angel's, and meeting me with the remark of, "Look at that and weep," showed me a diamond that weighed fifty-four carats, and worth £5,000, that his boy had just handed to him. The boy saw it roll down the heap of "cascalho" while shoveling it in the "Tom." It is of a yellowish tinge, of this size and shape; a perfect octohedron. He leaves for home to-day, as happy as a king.

25TH.—Washed out ten loads. No diamonds. Messrs. Parkes & Co., who are mining on the second kopie, Klip Drift side, had been working their claim for a month, and had found no diamonds. They had only a small corner to work to finish it, when they intended to leave for home, in disgust. They offered their claim to a neighbor for £1, but as the offer was refused, they concluded to finish it themselves. At the very first pick, a beautiful fifty-six carat diamond rolled out about the same shape as De Kock's, but of first water and flawless. It is valued at £10,000. Parkes come over and invited us to call and see it. Rawstorne went over and saw it, and has been feeling bad ever since; it makes him covetous. Webster found at his kopie a nine carat and a twenty-six carat diamond to-day. A singular-looking diamond of nineteen carats was found on the second kopie at Klip Drift. It is of a bright yellow color, free from specks or flaws, and quite flat; it is valued at £2,000. Over £20,000 worth of diamonds found to-day.

26TH.—Washed out nine loads, and found one diamond. I was offered a twenty-six carat diamond to-day for £700, but upon examining it closely, found that it was split nearly in two. Didn't bite! I purchased eleven diamonds to-day, all less than one carat each.

27TH.—We found one diamond to-day, weighing one-eighth of a carat, first water. As one of our boys wanted it, we let him have it for 10s.

28TH.—Attended a ball at Mr. Biddulph's tent; three ladies and forty gentlemen present; concluded not to dance; sat up till daylight discussing politics with the two Presidents, and washing it down occasionally with * * *

29TH.—About a dozen gentlemen who had come from Colesburg on a lark, and had been our guests for the last week, returned home to-day. They could not resist the temptation of mining a little themselves, and had found a diamond, for the ownership of which they played a game of seven up. We all had a regular square meal at Heathcote's tent before they left—boiled ham, roast mutton, mutton curry, plum pudding, * * * English ale, and a clean table-cloth.

SEPT. 1ST.—Saw a beautiful dodecahedron diamond, 1¾ carats, of a bright orange color; tried to purchase it, but the Dutchman would not sell. A trader named Franz Roose, who is mining and trading near Hebron, was awakened from his sleep at twelve o'clock last night by a Koranna native.

Thinking that he wanted liquor, he would not let him in; but finding that he had a diamond for sale, he got up and lit a candle, when the native rolled out of a dirty rag a magnificent sixty-three carat diamond. Roose was stunned for a minute, but recovering, asked the native what he wanted for it. He said that he wanted R.'s wagon and ox team, twenty other oxen, one hundred sheep, and £30 in coin. R. told him he could have it, and £20 worth of goods besides. R. was offered £5,000 for it; it had cost him £280. I saw the diamond to-day, and Roose told me the story. He says that the Koranna promises to tell him where he found it. It has a yellowish tinge on the outside, but it is not deep, and it may cut into a 35 cart brilliant, and fetch £10,000 in Europe.

2D.—Washed out fifteen loads to-day. *No diamonds.* A seventy-seven carat diamond was found on the old kopie at Klip Drift to-day. It is full of specks and flaws, and fit for boart only. Worth about £100. Mr. Unger showed me over two hundred diamonds that he had purchased lately, mostly large sized; one of forty carats. Mr. Robinson showed me a diamond of nine carats, that looked exactly like a crystal, and it had to be thoroughly tested before it was known to be a diamond.

On the 8th I left for Bloemfontein and the Colony, having to leave two-thirds of my claim unworked, and attend to my regular business. We found several other diamonds before I left.

CHAPTER VIII.

PNIEL (pronounced Peeneel) is situated on the east bank of the Vaal River, about 100 miles from its mouth. The diggings are about three miles from the mission station. The Vaal at the diggings is about 200 yards wide, and numerous yawl ferries are constantly plying to and from Klip Drift, or Parkerton, as it is now called. A large wagon ferry has also been started, to be used at high water, when the river cannot be forded. A high kopie rises at the drift, from which a rand or spur runs down and parallel with the river. This rand is about fifty feet high, and more than a mile long, and it is on the top and sides of this that the diamonds are found. Diamonds have been picked up from the top of the very highest kopie; but as none have been found there by mining, and as there is the remains of an old kraal or native hamlet still to be seen, it is presumed that the diamonds that were found on it were left there by the native children, who had picked them up from the surface of the rand, perhaps to play "Jack-stones" with. I have frequently wandered among the ruins of the kraal, looking for some of those lost "Jack-stones." The alluvial deposit on this rand is about a mile long, 200 yards wide, and from twelve to thirty feet deep. The first deposit from the surface, about six inches, is of a brownish color. The second deposit, of about five feet, is quite red, and the other strata is white. All these strata, or deposits, contain a large percentage of water-worn pebbles, ranging from a pea to an egg in size. The diamonds are found among these pebbles. The bed rock is quite flat, and very much water-worn wherever you strike it. There are about 3,000 inhabitants at Pniel at present; and although a great many leave for the new rushes, the place is gradually growing. There are stores, auction marts, saloons, billiard tables, bakers, butchers, doctors, lawyers, but no undertakers yet. But an enterprising acquaintance of mine has just started up with a nest of coffins on speculation, so that intending emigrants need have no fears of not being decently buried, in case they should want to remain there. A post-office has been established, and a newspaper, called the *Diamond News*, is successfully under way, and has six pages of news and advertisements; it is issued weekly (on Saturday). You can safely ship diamonds by post from here if you register them, and you can rely upon their being delivered to any part of the colony that you may wish to send them.

At these diggings more diamonds have been found than at any other district of the diamond fields, but they average small (about one carat). Nearly every miner who got a claim within the limits that I have described above, was sure to get diamonds, but they would be small, and, perhaps, not pay expenses. Still, as you will see by my diary, quite a number of large diamonds were reported, and perhaps a great number of "bulls" were found and not reported. A tax of 10s. a month on all miners for each cradle is now enforced at Pniel. This goes to the missionary society, but will hereafter go into the hands of the British Commissioner to be used, as occasion may require, at the mines. The claims allowed are thirty feet square, and will take an ordinary company of six four months to work out. The committee require that all miners shall sign the following rules for the miners and others of the Klip Drift Diggings:

1. That the rules be called "Rules for the miners and occupiers of the Klip Drift Diggings."
2. That the committee consist of seven (7) members.
3. That four members constitute a quorum, and that the chairman have a casting vote, in addition to his vote as committee-man; and in the absence of the permanent chairman, the members present to elect one from among themselves.
4. That from and after the 15th July, 1870, any person working or taking a claim will be required to pay to the committee the sum of two shillings and sixpence (2s. 6d.) which will entitle him to a digger's right here. This sum to be expended for local purposes, as stated in Rule No. 18; and any digger failing to comply with this rule will render himself liable to have his claim jumped.
5. That the extent of a claim shall not exceed twenty feet square, and any one holding ground in excess is liable to have the surplus jumped, the part to be indicated by the owner of such claim.
6. That no case or dispute will be entertained by the committee unless the complainant first deposit the sum of ten shillings (10s.) in the hands of the secretary, the same to be refunded, in the event of the judgment being in his favor; the loser to pay ten shillings (10s.)
7. That no person or persons will be allowed to slaughter animals within the precincts of the camp, but on application to the committee certain places will be pointed out by them for that purpose.
8. That any person or persons depositing night soil within the precincts of the camp will be fined, except at such places as the committee may point out.
9. That any person or persons discharging fire-arms within the camp, shall be subject to a penalty not exceeding £5.
10. That no person shall be allowed to serve natives with liquors on Sundays, except for their employers, and not then without a written order, under a penalty of not exceeding £5, and no person selling liquors will be permitted to keep their places of business open after 11 o'clock A.M.
11. That all dead carcasses of animals be removed to a distance of at

least half a mile from the precincts of the camp; in default of which the committee will have the same done at the expense of the owner of the cart.

12. That all thoroughfares be left free and uninterrupted.

13. That all persons having or requiring a stand for business purposes, shall pay to the committee the sum of twenty shillings (20s.) per month; such stand to be not more than fifty feet square, and no person will pe permitted to take possession of any plot of ground without the sanction of the committee, and in the event of such ground being required for digging purposes, it shall be competent for the committee to order the occupier to remove to some other spot, after giving due notice.

14. That no person or persons can convene a public meeting without sending a requisition, signed by at least twenty-five (25) diggers, to the committee, stating their reasons for wanting such meeting called.

15. That for every contravention of the foregoing regulations, for which no penalty has been provided, a fine not exceeding five pounds (£5) sterling will be imposed on conviction, recoverable as provided for in Rule No. 17.

16. That it be in the power of the committee to act in such cases as are not provided for in the foregoing rules.

17. That in the event of non-payment of a fine, the committee reserve to themselves the right of holding a sale of such property of the individual as shall cover the amount, and every digger will be expected to assist the committee in enforcing their decision.

18. That all moneys derived from claims, fines, and other sources, be expended in sanitary and other purposes necessary to the diggers of this place.

19. That every digger be required to sign the foregoing rules, and those failing to do so, will not be entitled to protection.

STAFFORD PARKER, President.

The claim adjoining mine has paid £4,000, and has not been half worked out. The largest diamond found on it sold for £1,700—I could not find out the weight of it; while a claim on the other side of mine did not pay expenses, although diamonds were found in it. There seem to be regular runs, which are only found by accident. These runs may not be more than two feet wide; but for ten feet on each side, not a single diamond will be found. Now, in Brazil and India, a regular diamond miner can tell the instant that he comes across a diamond run, and he will not waste his time in washing any other kind of soil. In Brazil, where small diamonds predominate, a miner who has been brought up to the business can tell the average yield of "cascalho" before washing it, like the silver miners of Mexico, who can tell the average value of a heap of ore, merely from the appearance of it.

Parkerton, formerly called Klip Drift, now named after Stafford Parker, who first let the world know of the existence of diamond mines there, and who has been president and leading man of that side of the river ever since, contains at present about two thousand white inhabitants, who mostly live in tents. Some have built frames in the shape of a house, which they cover over with canvas, having swinging doors and windows to them. Others had frame houses built at the colonial towns, and brought up in pieces on ox wagons; others brought corrugated iron houses, and at least half a dozen houses were built of unburnt brick. During a thunder storm that passed over the place a short time ago, almost every hut and house was leveled with the ground. Since then, they have been more substantially put up. The place is gradually assuming the shape of a laid-out town; the old mining roads have become streets. Town lots of about 100 feet square, have been taken up on the second, or Town Kopie, and walled in by those who chose to do so. In the main street, which runs parallel with the river, Mr. Parker has built a brick music hall, at which theatrical performances take place, and ventriloquists, minstrels, etc., give entertainments. There are half a dozen doctors, two diamond merchants, a photographer, two butchers' shops, two bakers', and about a dozen stores, where you can purchase groceries, drugs, clothes, hardware, boots and shoes, mining tools, and everything else that a miner requires. There are also several carpenters' and blacksmiths' shops; also two jewelers' shops, and drinking saloons, till you can't rest. The building of several churches is contemplated, and they will probably soon be up. At present, Divine service is held in the committee tent and billiard saloons, of which latter there are three; also at the music hall. Sunday is strictly observed; all the stores and saloons are closed, and large congregations assemble at the different services. There are about 250 women and children at Parkerton, which gives the place an air of civilization, especially on Sundays, when they come out in their best store clothes. Deacon

Kitton is there at present, establishing an English church. The climate at Parkerton is healthy, and, considering the manner in which people live, there is very little sickness. A slight fever prevails during the summer, but it seldom proves fatal. Occasionally they have terrific rain storms, accompanied by thunder and lightning. The government of Parkerton is carried on by Mr. Campbell, the magistrate appointed by the English Government. The miners will, no doubt, derive a greater benefit by having a strong hand to govern them, than by having a Republic of their own; at least till the place has become more settled. The Colonial Government has been very liberal to emigrants, and the colonists are anxious that a good class of emigrants should come out and settle in the Colony. Americans, especially, are thought very highly of on account of their energy and enterprise. The English language is the prevailing one at the mines, but there are a great many Dutch there who can not understand a word of English. The natives around Parkerton are called Korannas; they are of a dark mulatto hue, and not at all dangerous, being completely overawed by the number of white men at the mines, but they will steal if they get a chance. The best laborers come from the far north, on the Limpopo; they are called Kaffirs, and are quite black, and generally honest. Capt. Gordon and Mr. Green, at Pniel, have three of these blacks each, and they trust them altogether in mining, washing, and sorting; and I have frequently seen them hand their masters the diamonds that they had found perhaps the day before. Provisions can be bought at the following prices: beef, 3*d.* per lb.; mutton, 3*d.* per do.; butter, 2*s.* per do.; coffee, 1*s.* per do.; sugar, 4*d.* per do.; flour, 17*s.* per 100 lbs.; meal, 7*s.* per do.; potatoes, 4*s.* per do.; corn, 3*s.* per do. Forage for mules or horses, 6*d.* per bundle, or one feed; board and lodging at the hotels, 10*s.* per day; liquors, 6*d.* per drink. The photographer charges 20*s.* a dozen for *cartes-de-visite.* Small-size cradles are made for £2 10*s.*; Yankee Babies £2 10*s.*, and everthing else, including clothes and hardware, are as cheap as at the sea-ports. As at all new mining camps, the stores are generally overstocked with goods as soon as the rush commences, and the consequence is, that the prices soon go down. All the store-keepers will take diamonds for their goods, and will give the highest price for them that is given at the mines. The two diamond merchants also give very good prices in cash for all diamonds brought them.

CHAPTER IX.

The next important mining camp is Hebron, situated about twenty miles above Pniel, and on the west side of the Vaal River. There are several stores here, and about one thousand white men, women, and children. Among the traders there is one named Robinson, who has purchased over one hundred diamonds from natives, who have found them on the surface. He has, no doubt, made his fortune. Hebron has not turned out as many or as fine diamonds as Parkerton or Pniel, and there has not been as great a percentage of successful miners there as at the above places. No tax is demanded there yet, but the place has been under the authority of the Klip Drift Government, and is now within the jurisdiction of Mr. Campbell, the magistrate. Bloemhof, a village about one hundred miles above Pniel, and on the Free State side of the Vaal River, has produced some diamonds, but there are very few miners working there. Diamonds have been found on the surface by the natives all the way from Bloemhof to Pniel, but no rich deposit has been discovered yet except at Hebron; but there is no doubt that there are plenty of rich deposits somewhere between these places.

Webster's Kopie, three miles below Pniel, on the Free State side, has turned out a great many diamonds, mostly large ones. The largest known weighs about forty carats. Mr. Webster, who discovered this kopie, has made a fortune there, having fortunately struck the best part of it upon his arrival. The balance was immediately taken up by miners from the great camps, who rushed there upon finding out that Webster had made the discovery. Webster was entitled to four claims for opening the new mines; thus he secured the best part of the kopie.

Good Hope and New Hope are situated nearly opposite Webster's Kopie, on the west bank of the Vaal. At both these places a large number of diamonds were found, and rushes ensued from the great camps to them.

Gong Gong, another rich place, is situated fifteen miles below Pniel, on the west bank. The deposit extends over a great extent of ground, and at least five hundred miners are working here, and some rich deposits have been turned up.

Lucas Kopie, nearly opposite Gong Gong, on the Free State side, has proved exceedingly rich for such a small area. Captain Lucas and party are from Natal. Some of them were members of the Rolliston party, of Old Kopie celebrity. They came over to Pniel when the place was opened to all comers, and were doing very well at a claim near mine, when one morning we found that their camp and claim had been deserted. Upon inquiry, we found that a Koranna had informed Captain Lucas that he had found a diamond on the surface of a certain kopie sixteen miles down the river; so Captain L. rode down and examined the place. He liked it so well that he determined to move the whole company down at once. As his company could not hold the whole of the kopie, he got three other Natal companies to join him, making four companies of sixteen men, who would work the whole kopie on equal shares. So at midnight they packed up and started for the new diggings, passing through the camps as quietly as possible, so as not to be observed and cause a rush. By next day it was found out, and a rush was made; but they were too late. The Natalians had taken up all the claims that were worth anything. In six weeks the Natalians had taken out £80,000 worth of diamonds, one of them weighing 108 carats, and worth £40,000. This gave each £5,000 for his six weeks' work. The kopie is one mile and a half from the river, and they had to haul water to their claims, and wash the "cascalho" in a stretched ox hide, and with common hand sieves.

Cawood's Hope, near Lucus' Kopie, on the west bank, is now turning out an immense number of diamonds. There are about one thousand miners there now. The last and greatest rush has just taken place to Sifonel, about twenty-five miles below Parkerton, on the west bank. This is where Jautjie, the paramount chief of the whole of the diamond district on the west bank, resides. At least two thousand miners are working there now, and it has turned out immensely rich.

An American named Bebell, whose father (a retired sea captain) is residing now in Brooklyn, N. Y., has been business agent and secretary to this chief for several years. He has been trading with the natives for ivory and ostrich feathers, and when diamonds were first discovered he frequently purchased them from the natives. He went up to Klip Drift and Hebron while the Natal and King William's Town parties were hunting for the deposits of diamonds, but left before the mines were discovered. Before leaving, however, he obtained from Jautjie a concession of all the country on the west bank that Jautjie claimed, for thirty years, giving £750 for this privilege, and five per cent. on all taxes that Bebell might collect from miners working on the fields, in case the mines should be discovered. Bebell then loaded his wagon with goods and started on a trading expedition, more especially to trade with the natives for diamonds. He followed the west bank of the Vaal down to its mouth, and then the Orange River to the mouth of the great Haarte Beeste River. He found similar soil to that at Klip Drift all the way down. After leaving the Haarte Beeste River, the country changed to a sandy soil, covered with bushes. He then struck off the Orange River in a northerly direction, going as far as lat. 25° south. He then came in a southerly direction near to the mouth of the Orange River, and leaving his wagon at Kookfontein, walked over to Port Nolloth, on the Atlantic, and took a schooner for Capetown. He had not heard from the diamond district for six months, and he was astonished to learn that during his absence the mines had been discovered and a great rush made, and that there were one thousand white men finding diamonds at Sifonel, where he had been living for several years. He immediately issued the following proclamation, and started for the mines :

"Proclamation.—Diamond Diggers, Take Notice!—
I, David Bebell, do hereby give notice that I am legally authorized to grant licenses to parties desiring to dig for diamonds and other precious stones within the territory of Yarki Mothebe (Jautjie), paramount chief of the Batlapene Nation, which territory lies on the west side of the Vaal River.

"The right was granted me by concession, dated May 20th, 1870, by the said chief and his councillors. Application for licenses to be made at Lekatlong, the residence of the chief. The charge for individual licenses will be 2s. 6d. sterling per month."

If his claim is upheld by the British Government, he will charge the miners 2s. 6d. a month only for license to mine, and Bebell will make his everlasting pile.

About thirty miles from Pniel, in a southerly direction, and ten miles from the Vaal, on the Free State, there is a farm of over six hundred acres that has turned out rich in diamonds. Five hundred small ones have been picked up from the surface. It was purchased from the Dutch owner by a company from the Colony for £2,000, and they are making preparations to work it on a large scale. About a month ago two hundred miners went down from the great camp and jumped it; but the owners called upon the Free State Government for protection, and they sent a command to Bulfontein, and the miners left without resistance.

Jagersfontein is the name of another diamondiferous farm near Faursmith, owned by a family named Visser. They have allowed about fifty Dutch families to mine on the farm and wash at the dam, and they have turned out a large number of diamonds, among them one that weighed over fifty carats. The Visser family get one-fourth of the proceeds of all the finds. The head of the family is a widow, fat, not fair, but fully forty. Any nice young man, that thinks he is fascinating and irresistible enough, had better come out and marry that farm.

There are many other farms where diamonds have been found upon the surface, and perhaps many others where they have not originally been found there, but salted to catch some unwary speculator. There is no doubt but that one thousand kopies will yet prove rich in diamonds, and a thousand fortunes made; but still, there will be a thousand men who will fail even in making a living at diamond mining. As yet it is all chance; after a while, when men become better acquainted with the geology of the country, they will have a better chance of success. Large companies, who will work a whole farm systematically, are sure of success.

JAGERSFONTEIN.—The following is an extract from a private letter: "On coming to this farm, you come through a small port, and a large basin surrounded by kopies meets your view. From the kopies to the present claims is a gradual descent, which leads me to think that the diamonds now found must, at some time or other, have been washed to their present resting places. No pretty pebbles here; the gravel is of the commonest description, and full of garnets, green stone, and carbon. In digging, when no more gravel can be found, the claim is given up, as diamonds are only found in the gravel. Each claim pays £2 per month, and you can dig where you like, and open as many different places as you think proper. . . . Each claim is twenty feet square. At present my hole is about twelve feet deep, and after all the gravel is taken out of the sides and bottom, and no more gravel, we sink another one alongside, and so on till the claim is worked out. For the first three feet nothing is met with but black pot clay, and then red pot clay, which continues till you get to gravel; and if no gravel, rotten sand of a greenish color, when the digger finds that it is of no use going further, and tries his luck at some other spot. To show you how the nature of the soil varies: a farmer from Fort Beaufort took the next claim to mine, and went down ten feet without finding the least sign of gravel, and consequently gave up his claim and looked for another one; while in mine, from the first four feet down to twelve, I found lots of gravel, with every chance of its continuance. From the pit the gravel is thrown up on the sifting floor, and dry sifted in an ordinary lime sieve, fine; it is then thrown into a bread tin, with small holes in the bottom, and held in a half cask containing water, the gravel well rubbed with the hand; it is then placed in another half cask adjoining, and well washed in the pan, the water drained off, and then the contents placed on my table, where I sort. I have four posts driven into the ground, over the top of which I have a white cotton sheet to keep the sun off, and under this I sit, in front of my sorting-table, from six o'clock in the morning till six in the evening, allowing one hour for breakfast and another for dinner; so you will see that I am not idle. In sorting, with a little practice, you can go through a deal of gravel in a day. With a small piece of iron, with the turn of the hand, you bring before you some dozens of stones at once, and at a single glance can see if there is a diamond or not, and if the latter, sweep off sharp; and so on till your day's work is finished."

EXPLANATION OF WASHING MACHINE.

The washing cradle consists of a chest of drawers on rockers, generally about three feet six inches in height and two feet six inches in length, and two feet in breadth. The hopper is twelve inches in height, and by its spread makes the receptacle for "cascalho" one foot each way wider than the cradle. The drawers are made of teak wood, to prevent them from swelling when wet. The sides of these drawers are three inches high, and a space of three inches is left between each drawer, to allow of a small rake to be introduced for the purpose of stirring the washed pebbles occasionally. The pieces of wood that the drawers slide upon should be one inch wide, and reach from the top of one drawer to the bottom of the one above, making a close fit, so that the pebbles can not get in between their sides and choke up the drawers so that they could not be drawn out. The top drawer should be sheet iron, with half or five-eight inch holes about an inch apart. All the pebbles that do not pass through these holes can be readily examined and thrown aside without emptying them on a table. The second drawer must have a wire bottom, with the holes half an inch in size, and the bottom drawers must be made of one-sixteenth inch wire mesh. All that will pass through this last sieve will not pay to sort. The last two drawers are emptied on a table for sorting. Any kind of a pump will do that can throw three inches of water through the hose to the top of the sluice, where the dirt is placed and washed into the cradle. They generally put about ten shovelsful in at a washing, and this takes about five minutes to wash.

EXPLANATION OF DRY SIFTER, OR "YANKEE BABY."

The dry sifter is set in a frame made of four-inch scantling, well and strongly lined with cross-pieces. The sifting machine is hung in this frame on straps. At the rear the machine is three inches high, and at two feet from the rear it widens to one foot in height, thus giving the desired inclination to both sieves, so that the "cascalho" can easily drop off at either end. The top sieve consists of one-eighth inch wire, placed one inch apart, and crossed with wire at the same distances. The lower sieve is of one-sixteenth inch wire mesh, and allows only the fine sand to pass through it. Now, the lower and upper sieve are held together with firm sides of plank, and are consequently shaken together from side to side. One miner shovels in the "cascalho" at the top sieve, which is protected by a hopper, while another shakes it, and watches the large pebbles pass out, to see that no "bulls," or large diamonds, escape. The pebbles under an inch in size pass through into the one-sixteenth inch sieve, and all but the fine gravel and sand passes to the front and empties on the ground ready for carting to the river. The coarse gravel and fine sand are left on the ground, and generally amount to from one-half to two-thirds of the "cascalho" dug out, and there is that much less hauling saved, and the washing is also facilitated by getting rid of the fine sand that helps to clog up the lower sieve. The drawing is on the scale of one inch to the foot, and is the average and best size for the machine. It is in general use at the mines during dry weather, but in wet it is useless, and all the "cascalho" has to be hauled to the river and washed. The wood work is generally made of the yellow wood of South Africa.

DRY SIFTER.

Two views of the Dry Sifter or Yankee Baby

Front view

Side view

CHAPTER X.

There are several ways of washing for diamonds in South Africa, and they seem to be a decided improvement on the Brazilian system. After the "cascalho" is dug from the mines, it is sifted. The very coarse stones, or those larger than, say, a cubic inch, are thrown to one side, and the very fine gravel and sand passes through the sieve, and is also thrown on one side. The middlings, or all gravel, from one-sixteenth of a cubic inch to an inch are then hauled down to the river for washing, or washed at the mine. The dry sifting used to be done with a common meal-sieve, or a two-handed square one that was invented later; two men would use this while another would shovel in. I then invented a machine which has been universally copied, and which the miners christened the "Yankee Baby;" and one man could sift with this machine as much in ten hours as four could with the common sifter. (This machine is described elsewhere.) The miners generally rise at break of day, and dig, sift, and cart till 9 A.M., when they have breakfast. At 10 A.M. they commence to wash and sort at the river or at the mine; one person rocks the cradle, while another pours in water that he dips with a pail from the river. The rocker then sorts the stones in the upper sieve, and empties the pebbles from the middle and bottom sieves on a common table, where they are carefully sorted or examined by the sorters. A scraper, similar to a knife, is used to spread out a handful of gravel from the pile. This is looked over for an instant, and then scraped off, and another batch scraped from the pile for examination. After the first diamond is found, which causes a peculiarly pleasant sensation to the finder, who, seeing how easily they are recognized at first sight, is enabled to sort very rapidly, without fear of losing any diamonds; some, however, go a little too fast after a while, and scrape off the diamonds and lose them. Mr. Unger saw a man scrape off an eight carat diamond one day from his table. He then picked it up and gave him over £100 for it. I knew of an instance where a Dutchman, who had paved his tent with washed pebbles, picked out three diamonds from it that had been scraped off the table by some careless sorter. Some of the miners, especially the Dutch, get a gre n ox hide, and lace the edges to a square frame; set this frame upon four legs at the mine, and fill the hide with stones to stretch it bowl-shape. After it was sufficiently stretched they would haul water from the river and wash the "cascalho" in it with a common meal-sieve, having previously dry-sifted it. They would then sort the washed pebbles. The sieves used were $\frac{1}{16}$ or $\frac{1}{12}$ of an inch mesh. This was a very slow way of getting on. The men could not get more than about one cart-load a day dug and washed, while with the rocker at the river two men could get through three loads a day. With our machines, pump, and hose, two white men and five boys, we could get through fifteen cart-loads a day. About six feet frontage is allowed at the river for each cradle or machine. The sorting is the most monotonous part of the work, and five boys will wash enough in four hours to keep three men sorting ten hours. At 1 o'clock the work is knocked off for tiffin or lunch. At 4 o'clock the washers cease, and go to mining for next day's washing. Some of the miners cart their "cascalho" during moon-light nights to the river ready for washing next day; but in winter it is too cold to wash earlier than 9 A.M. Some of the miners have a regular Californian "longtom" and an Australian pump. The pump is made of four pieces of plank, twelve feet long by four inches wide; a common leather suction is placed on the end of a long pole and inserted into this tube. The pump is then placed in a reclining position, with one end in the river and the other over the upper end of the tom. One man, with a long, regular stroke, can keep a constant stream of three inches running, while two men are kept constantly raking the "cascalho" backward and forward, till the water runs clear; then they take the washed stuff out by the shovelful and put it on the sorting-table. I do not approve of this plan, as the raking can be dispensed with by rocking, and thus two movements saved, making it less tiresome to the miner; and there is always danger of small diamonds being washed away. Pumps are also used for supplying the cradles with water, instead of buckets, and it is much the best way, as they give a steady supply. At 6 P.M. the miners knock off work and dine; after which some would write, some would make their purchases of provisions, and others would go to the main camp and play billiards, black-pool, or unlimited loo; others would hunt up the diamond merchants and sell their finds, or go to the store where they had diamond scales and weigh them, if they intended to keep them for the European market.

Parties from America do not require to purchase much in that country. Californian long-handled shovels and picks are the only things that can not be had here yet, but a supply of these articles will soon find their way here, no doubt. If they come *via* England they can obtain most of their supplies there at a much cheaper rate than in America. You can obtain an outfit in any of the South African ports much cheaper than in America, but not so cheap as in England. Wagons, oxen, mules, and horses must be purchased in Africa. No foreign wagon will stand the climate. I was foolish enough to purchase a wagon in England. I had it made of ash, very strongly, and shipped it to Natal in 1869. I got about 500 miles into the interior, when it broke down so completely that I had to give up the expedition, and get back to the coast the best way I could. Tents that sell in England, at Edgington's, No. 2 Duke Street, London Bridge, for £5, sell in Capetown for £8, and in America for about £10. They are nine feet, regular house-shaped. The following is the necessary outfit for four men, this number being best to start with from America, as it lessens the expenses of each, and they can divide into two companies at the mines and hire native labor:

Either an ox wagon and 14 oxen, or a spring wagon and 6 mules	£150
A nine-foot tent	5
A Scotch cart, 2 mules, or 4 oxen	40
Six months' provisions	50
A set of mining tools	5
A set of carpenters' tools	3
A diamond washer	3
A dry-sifter	2

SOUTH AFRICAN DIAMOND FIELDS.

Cooking utensils	£3
100 feet of 12-inch planking	2
	£263
Passage from America, first-class	120
	£383

or say £100 each. Now, there is a cheaper way than the above, by taking second-class passage from America, and then by paying passage from the African sea-port to the diamond fields, thus avoiding the heavy cost of a wagon and team; but the advantage of having a team of your own is, that you are not necessarily confined to the great mining camps, but can go a long way from them and prospect on new grounds, and perhaps strike on a new and rich kopie that has never been discovered before. The expense of the cheaper plan would be as follows for four men:

Passage to the mines from sea-ports of Africa	£40
A Scotch cart and 4 oxen at the mines	50
A tent	5
Mining tools	5
Cooking utensils	2
A few carpenter's tools	1
A common washing cradle	2
A dry sifter	2
Second-class passage from America, £20 each	80
Lumber, say about	2
	£189

or say £50 each. The necessary clothing is of course not included in the above, but a miner must have two suits of strong corduroy (colored), one suit of plain clothes for Sundays and other occasions, two pairs of nail-studded navvy boots, one pair walking boots, one heavy pea-jacket, two sets of underclothing, four woolen overshirts, four pairs woolen socks, a single mattress and pillow (hair is best); have the mattress and pillow covered with a colored cotton slip that can be taken off and washed; two double blankets, towels, toilet necessaries, sewing materials, a few medicines such as quinine, anti-bilious pills, castor oil, etc.; a leather belt, a sporting rifle and ammunition; and a marine glass is also very useful in looking out for game or lost cattle. Diamond scales are also necessary for those who contemplate purchasing or selling diamonds, or who intend to prospect at a distance from the main camp. It is well to learn how to take the specific gravity of the diamond before leaving home. There ought to be at least one watch in the company, and a small mariner's compass for exploring parties.

I would advise no one to come to this country unless they have a capital, or can stand hard work; and not even the better class if they do not have means to give them a year's outfit, and in case of failure to take them home again. It is the worst place in the world for a penniless man to come to. He cannot get work, nor can he get a passage home again; and the best thing he can do is to drown himself, or steal something and be sent to the breakwater, where he will be provided for by the State. To men of means who are seeking a chance for investment, I will say that there are splendid opportunities for it, not only at the diamond mines, but all through the Colony, the adjacent republics, and the Portuguese settlements.

CHAPTER XI.

Six months after the previous chapters were written, I concluded to return to the diamond fields and give them another trial. I went up this time by the Inland Transportation Company's wagon, drawn by eight horses. There were eleven other passengers besides myself; among them three ladies who were going to the fields to join their husbands and brothers. There were also three ex-English officers, who had sold out their commissions and were bound for the diamond fields to try their luck. Wagon, passengers, and twenty pounds of baggage for each were put upon the railway train bound to Wellington, fifty miles above Capetown, where we were landed in a few hours, and inspanning eight fine horses, started over the mountain road to Klip Drift, 700 miles distant. Arrived at a pretty town called "Ceres"

THE HOUSE IN WHICH DIAMONDS WERE FOUND.

at 8 P.M., and we obtained good bed and board till 6 A.M. next morning, when we resumed our journey, generally getting good board and beds every night; passing successively through the towns of Beaufort West, Victoria West, and Hopetown, and arriving at Pniel and Klip Drift on the afternoon of the twelfth day. I found upon my arrival at Pniel and Klip Drift that extensive alterations had taken place in both towns. There were more substantial buildings up, built of stone, brick, iron, and wood, mostly stores, doing a wholesale business with the neighboring camps up and down the river and inland. But there were not one-tenth as many miners as were here when I left; most of them had gone up and down the rivers after working out their claims here. Just at this present moment a great rush had been made about twenty miles down the river, below Cawood's Hope, and on the Klip Drift side of the Vaal. I went down there, and found that there were at least 5,000 diggers mining among the huge bowlders on a flat that is covered with water from the river. During the rainy season, the claims are quite shallow, and a thirty-foot claim does not last longer than from one to two months, while at Pniel the claims last from six to twelve months. When I returned to Pniel, where I stopped at a very good hotel that had lately been put up, "Jardine's," I learned of a new inland deposit that had just been discovered. About six months ago, a Dutchman, named Du Toit, while sitting in front of his mud-plastered house, discovered a small diamond sticking in the plaster. He aroused himself with an effort from his normal state of laziness, and continued his search around the house, and discovered in all seventeen small diamonds. After a few days' thought, he remembered having, some years ago, made this plaster from mud gathered near his dam; and thither he and his family went, about one hundred yards from the house, and getting on their hands and knees, discovered quite a number of small diamonds, all the way from one-sixteenth to one carat in size. Lillienfield and Webb, two diamond merchants, purchased this farm from Du Toit for £2,000 in "bluebacks" (Orange Free State currency), and set about fifty men working on it, and up to this time they had taken out over 500 diamonds, the largest, however, not being over five carats in weight.

A rush was soon made from the river diggings for this place, called Bulfontein, and some five hundred diggers jumped the claims and commenced to work them on their own account, in spite of the protests of the owners. Finally the owners prevailed on the State authorities to send a command of one thousand armed men to run the jumpers off. Upon the approach of this body the jumpers fled, some of them to the next farm, called "Du Toit's Pan," and while prospecting, found a deposit there also. They immediately jumped this farm and organized a committee, who laid out claims of thirty feet square, and the miners commenced work. A great rush immediately ensued, and in two months there were 20,000 miners and their families there. Water was scarce, hardly enough for drinking, and the "cascalho" had to be sifted and worked dry. Lillienfield and Webb soon managed to purchased this farm also, and as they saw that the miners were determined to remain in spite of them and the "comando," they concluded not to try and get them off, but to let them remain if they would pay Lillienfield and Webb 10s. 6d. per month for each claim. The mirers consented, and went back to Bulfontein and jumped it again, on the same terms. The two deposits join now, and contain about two thousand claims, which, with the rents from town lots in the camps, yield the proprietors not less than £1,000 per month net.

Soon after this, diamonds were discovered on another farm adjoining Du Toit's Pan, called De Been's Farm. This proved to be richer still than either Bulfontein or Du Toit's Pan. An acquaintance of mine found over 150 diamonds in two months, some of them over sixteen carats in weight. At all the above places diamonds were found, weighing from 30 to 127 carts; this last was found in a claim fronting my tent at Du Toit's. The Dutch farmer who dug it out commenced dancing and hollering, and soon raised a large crowd around him. He jumped upon his sorting-table, and holding up the diamond, showed it to the crowd. It was truly a monster. Then jumping down again, he made a straight line for his tent, and striking it, gathered up his household gods, inspanned his oxen, and left for home, saying that he had enough, and that any one who chose could have his claim. That claim was jumped instanter, but I never heard of another diamond being found in it, although they were being found every day in the adjoining claims. A ninety carat diamond was found next to mine at Bulfontein, also by a Dutchman. By this time there were 30,000 people at the three farms, and quite a town had sprung up at each camp, full of canteens and stores, billiard and bowling saloons. Over 1,000 females are in camp, and on Sunday they are all out-going to the different churches, dressed in their store clothes, and gay store clothes they are too.

About the 1st of August, 1871, my former partner at Pniel, Fleetwood Rawstorne, sent a negro to herd his cattle at a place where there was an abundance of green grass, one and a half miles from De Been's claims, where R. was mining very successfully. The native, while sitting under a tree, picked up a small diamond, and upon his return to camp he told his master of the discovery, and the next morning R. and his company went over there and laid out claims. It was soon reported at the different camps, and a general rush was made, and in two days over 800 claims were taken up. This place proved to be the richest deposit that was ever known in the world; the claims rose rapidly in price; thirty foot claims were divided into half and quarter claims, and these parts were sold to newcomers for from £25 to £500 per quarter claim. The deposit seemed to have no bottom. Before I left, some had sunk to a depth of seventy feet, and found diamonds every day all the way down, striking water at this depth, but no bed rock. I have known quite a number of miners to find from *five to twelve diamonds a day*, and they generally run large, some as high as ninety carats in weight. When I left in October, there were 5,000 people there, 75 per cent. of them doing well. There were as many as four different companies working a full claim, and none of the claims were more than one-third worked out. The place is named De Been's New Rush, or Colesburg Kopie.

CHAPTER XII.

Du Toit's Pan, De Been's, and Bulfontein are about twenty-four miles south of Klip Drift, and sixteen miles from the nearest point on the Vaal River. As there is no water to be had but from the dams that the Dutch farmers have built to collect rain water in, the "cascalho" has to be worked dry. The Vaal River is 180 feet lower than the deposit of diamonds at the above three camps, and consequently a canal can not be cheaply built to furnish water enough to wash the diamondiferous soil.

The deposits of diamondiferous soil are generally in what appear to be the craters of extinct volcanoes, filled up even with the top, surmounted with a ledge or rim of rock slate. At De Been's New Rush, this deposit consists of, first, a layer of light sand, containing but few diamonds; then a deposit of red clay that contains a few diamonds; then a thick bed of carbonate of lime, containing a great many diamonds; and last, a very thick deposit of decomposed green stone, that contains the greatest quantity, the largest and best quality of the precious gems. I know of one party who has gone down in his claim over seventy feet, and has found diamonds all the way down to the bottom, where he has struck water in small quantities.

These apparent craters are generally from 200 to 500 yards in diameter, and contain from 800 to 1,200 thirty-feet claims; 7½ feet of every other claim is reserved for a road that is used by carts that haul off the refuse from the claims after it has been sifted. This refuse contains a large number of hard lumps of carbonate of lime, that have been found too hard to break readily, so are thrown aside and carted off to the adjoining plain, and dumped as useless. Rains have come afterward, and, decomposing these lumps, disclosed diamonds to the fortunate passer-by. A native found one of fifty carats while passing one of these heaps, that had been washed out of a lump by the rain. Any machine that could be invented to crush these lumps quickly and cheaply, and

SKETCH OF MY OWN CLAIM AT THE DRY DIGGINGS.

not crush the diamonds that might be contained in them (for a diamond will crush), will be insured a large fortune at the fields.

The manner of mining at the dry diggings is as follows: Usually a company consists of two white men and four natives. It takes the four natives all their time to dig and sift out enough dirt to keep the two white men sorting. The negroes dig out the soil (there are no large stones like at the river), and laying it in a basin that they cut in the claim, pound it with a heavy sledge, to break up as many lumps as they can; they then shovel it into a coarse hand-screen, the wires of which are about one inch apart, and shake it through, throwing all the lumps aside to be carted away, then shoveling the balance into an oblong sieve, three feet long by two feet wide, the sieving of which is made of No. 18 wire, the holes being one-eighth of an inch in size. After shaking the fine stuff through this last sieve, all that remains in it is emptied on a common board table, where the sorters are; each sorter has a table-knife-shaped instrument in his right hand, and from the pile he scrapes about a handful, spreads it out with one sweep, and tells in an instant if there are any diamonds in it or not; if there are none, he throws it off, and repeats this all day. It is not hard work, but rather monotonous. The moment a diamond is found, at least a dozen diamond merchants will be after it, and you can sell your gem for gold instantly; or if you prefer you can ship them to Europe through the numerous merchants who have their branch houses at the different camps, and who generally give an advance on such consignments if wanted. Fine diamonds (first water) are still keeping up their prices in spite of the immense finds of South Africa. In fact, the demand for fine diamonds far exceeds the supply; it is only bad diamonds that have gone down in price about 25 per cent.

The health of the dry diggings is just the same as at the river; only four months in the year is the place unhealthy, and is mostly fatal to the intemperate only. Eight months of the climate is delightful, and splendid for persons suffering with pulmonary diseases. There are plenty of doctors and druggists at the mines. I insert an extract here from the *Diamond News,* published at Du Toit's Pan, December 16, 1871. The unhealthy months are December, January, February, and March only. At the three camps mentioned there are about 50,000 inhabitants:

"HEALTH OF THE FIELDS.—As the death rate at the fields has lately been very much overstated by correspondents, we have taken the trouble to ascertain from the Sanitary Inspectors the number of interments this month. At Du Toit's Pan and Bulfontein, from the 1st to the 20th inclusive, 40; Colesburg Kopie, between the 6th and 16th instant, 18; the average number of deaths at the three camps being about four per diem, which is a very small percentage. Still, however, there is a good deal of sickness, and every day, as the heat becomes intensified, parties are seen 'treking' for their respective homes."

The English Government have control of the diamond fields, and maintain good order. They have a force of six hundred cavalry in the district; they are called mounted police. Only one riot of any consequence has occurred at the fields.

I will now give my own experience and views as a diamond miner at the dry diggings. Upon my arrival at Du Toit's Pan I met two Americans, who, having landed at Capetown with but £5 between them, walked all the way to the mines, 700 miles. I immediately formed a partnership with them, and purchasing an outfit and a claim, turned the latter over to them to work; they to give me half they find, and I to furnish laborers and provisions. I formed several other companies on the same plan, some with English and others with Americans. For two months my income just covered my expenses. At the end of this time I closed up with my other companies and purchased a claim at De Been's New Rush, or Colesburg Kopie, for £50, and turned it over to the first two Americans who had walked from Capetown, they to give me half the proceeds of the find. They have been finding every day since they commenced on this new claim, and have turned out over 150 diamonds, among them a ten carat, sixteen carat, forty-two carat, and an eighty-three and a half carat, the balance running down to a quarter carat, including two, four, five, seven, and eight carats; and on January 1st, 1874, only one-third of the claim has been worked out; so that my second venture has proved a success, when my first on the Vaal was a failure. As I stated before, my advice to persons thinking of going to the diamond fields is as follows: None should think of starting with less than $1,000 in gold. Take a sailing vessel from New York or Boston; land either at Capetown or Port Elizabeth, and leave enough money with some merchant to pay their fare home if they fail at the diamond fields in a year's trial. It is not necessary to purchase anything that they will need anywhere else than at the diamond fields. By this means they will be rid of the trouble of carrying baggage, and can go up in the fast transports from Capetown or Port Elizabeth, in which they are allowed to carry only twenty pounds of baggage. Persons of more means can go to South Africa much quicker by steamer *via* England; it will take about forty-five days by this route; by sailing vessel it takes from sixty to eighty days.

CHAPTER XIII.

Capetown.—Having determined to start, one of the first inquiries made by the intending digger will be as to the best port in South Africa to make for. I think I shall best furnish that information by giving a description of the various points of disembarkation. Capetown, from its geographical position, its importance, and its being the seat of Government, I shall deal with first. Capetown is situated on the shores of Table Bay, in lat. 34° 22″ S., and long. 18° 24″ E. By reference to a map of South Africa, it will be found that almost at the southern extremity of the Continent, and on its western side, is a peninsula indented on the east by False Bay, and on the west by Table Bay. At the southern point of this land is the famous Cape of Good Hope celebrated for its storms, and the doubling of which has been so great an anxiety to many a mariner. Capetown is to the westward of this cape, so passengers who land at Table Bay will have no experience of the doubling or the storms. The harbor is an excellent anchorage, and one of the handsomest sheets of water in the world. It forms almost a complete circle, and is naturally sheltered from all storms but those from the north-west. In the winter seasons these storms rage with great fury, and in years gone by shipwrecks in this bay were so frequent that it was with great reluctance shipowners allowed their vessels to visit this port. The colonists, recognizing the necessity for improving the harbor, took the opportunity of Prince Alfred's visit to the colony in 1860 to commence extensive harbor works. These works are now concluded, and were declared open by H. R. H. the Duke of Edinburgh in 1870, just eight years after his Royal Highness had tipped the first wheelbarrow load into the sea. The works consist of breakwater and docks. The breakwater is 1,870 feet in length, and completely shelters the dock and the bay from north-westerly gales. Docks cover ten and a-half acres, and the whole of it was hewn out of the solid rock. The entrance is 100 feet wide and twenty-four feet deep. The widest part is 510 feet, and the length of the largest quay is 1,100 feet. The dock, it is unnecessary to say, is of the greatest convenience to shippers and shipowners. Since its opening it has been well patronized, and the revenue received from it gives a first-class return for the expenditure incurred, which amounts to close on a million pounds. In none of the British Colonies is there a harbor work to be compared to this. The town is laid out in Table Valley, and is completely inclosed on the east, south, and west by a mountainous cordon, consisting of the Devil's Peak, Table Mountain, and a singular formation known as Cape Lion, and which is supposed to be suggestive of a lion resting. Table Mountain, the highest of the cordon, is 3,582 feet above the level of the sea. It rises up from the valley, straight as a wall, and with its clearly cut ridges stands boldly out from the sky. From the sea, on a fine day, it is singularly imposing. "Under the shadow of Table Mountain," as the colonists themselves express it, is Capetown, the metropolis of South Africa. It was founded by Van Riebeck in 1652, taken by the English in 1796, restored again to the Batavian Government, and in 1803, at the peace of Amiens, it was given up to England once more, and has ever since been under her government: of course it must be understood that with Capetown the Cape Colony was also handed over. The colony, as I first mention it, was only a small patch of ground in Table Valley, but since that time its boundary has been extended north to the Orange River, and east to the Great Kei and Indive, and covers an area of about 350,000 square miles. Round and in Capetown the early Dutch settlers founded their houses; many of their descendants still live on the old farms, and while the town still shows evidence of the old style of Dutch architecture, it has some very handsome buildings, shops, and stores of modern designs, and which would not disgrace some of the wealthy capitals of Europe and America. The population of the town is put down at between thirty and forty thousand, while that of the whole colony is estimated by the census of 1865 at 496,381 souls; of these, 181,592 are white or European, 81,598 Hottentot, 100,536 Kaffir, 132,655 other colored. In Capetown there are but few Kaffirs, a few more Hottentots or Mozambiques, while the Malay population probably number one-third of the inhabitants of the place. The Malays are frugal, cleanly, sober; they drink no spirituous liquors and make excellent servants. The Dutch element is the preponderating European one in the town, while the energy, the enterprise, and the commercial reputation is sustained by the English and some Americans and a few of other nationalities. The town is laid out in blocks with a painful regularity (that is, the center of the town), while the houses and hovels of the poorer classes nestle close under the slopes of the mountain. There are several landing places in the harbor, and from the one known as the central wharf, there can be seen the splendid avenue of oaks known as the Government Gardens. These gardens are about a mile in length, having on one side the Botanical Gardens, which are elegantly laid out and well stocked with the choicest plants, and kept in creditable order. Facing the Botanical Gardens, and on the opposite side of the avenue, is the town residence of his Excellency the Governor. At the entrance to the garden is the most remarkable building in

4

Capetown; it incloses the museum and the library. It is a vast structure, of an elegant architectural design, with peristyle, but of which the façade is still unfinished. On entering the building by the principal doorway, to which a large and handsome flight of steps lead you, the visitor finds himself in a sort of vestibule decorated with some pictures and statues. To the right is the library, while the museum occupies the left wing of the building. In it can be found specimens giving a natural history of the colony, and a very fine collection of birds, beasts, etc. The library consists of 30,000 volumes of books, and some private rooms at the end of the library contain a very magnificent collection of works presented to the colony by a previous governor, Sir George Grey. This present is calculated to be worth £10,000—a royal gift, certainly. Besides this building, there are others. In the center of the town, on a square known as the Parade, is the Commercial Exchange. Then we have the South African College, the Somerset Hospital, Railway Station, Gas House, Bank Buildings, Public Offices, Supreme Court, Cathedral, Parliament House, and a number of other institutes too numerous here to mention. Strange to say, there is no theater in the town, although the community is very fond of theatrical entertainments. Some years ago a Mr. Sefton Parry had a company here for about three years, and made a handsome fortune. He has now the Holborn Theater, one of the newest and handsomest in London. Behind the town and toward the mountains are the residences of the merchants, surrounded by vineyards and fruit gardens. This part of the town is known as "The Gardens," and the residences are generally occupied by the Dutch or Africanders. These houses, nestling among the foliage, the light patches of green vineyards, the darker green of the oak, with the still darker green of the fir plantation, give a back-ground to Capetown, from a seaward point of view, both interesting and refreshing to the eye of the passenger after a long voyage. The English merchant, true to the traditions he brings with him from his native land, has his country residence, and this is either situated at Mowbray, Rondebosch, Claremont, or Wynberg, villages respectively at three miles, five miles, six miles, and eight miles from Capetown. They are reached either by rail or road, both of which skirt round the slope of the mountain amid avenues of trees and through vineyards and tastefully-arranged fruit and flower gardens. There are no spots I know of more desirable for residences than these places, perfectly sheltered by the forests of trees from the wind, the heat, and the sun. They are in winter protected from the heavy northerly gales, and in summer from the glaring, dazzling heat, so painful in the city. What the hills are to the East Indian merchant, these spots are to the merchants of Capetown.

The scenery is charming, but I have no time to give descriptions of scenery; my duty is to provide stern facts for the guidance of the emigrants. I must not forget, however, to mention that there are marine residences at Sea Point; this is the skirting of the Lion's Hill, and the villas have a view seaward, and a tramway, which runs every hour in the day, making these residences getatable and convenient. Before I leave Capetown I will mention that Parliament meets here annually. The Parliament consists of two representative bodies called the Legislative Council and the House of Assembly. The former is known as the upper and the latter as the lower House. The Council consists of twenty-one members elected for ten years; the House of Assembly of sixty-six members who are elected for five years. The session is supposed to last for fifty days, and for that number of days the members of the Assembly are allowed £1 per day, and an extra allowance of 1s. per mile for traveling expenses. The sessions last, however, much more than fifty days, and the debates are generally very earnest and exciting, although they are not so far advanced as Australia, where horsewhipping sometimes occurs during debate, or in America, where bowie knives and revolvers are not entirely ignored. The environs of Capetown are celebrated for Cape wine, and really to know what wine is produced in the country one must visit the Cape. I wonder how much colonial wine we drink at home fondly believing it is genuine Oporto or Madeira? Cape wine has long been a standing joke in the European and American markets, but that it has been allowed to remain so can only be explained by our gullability and ignorance. At Constantia, for instance, which is only half an hour's drive from the Wynberg railway station, and one of the prettiest drives one can well imagine, the wine vaults are splendid. Of course no one visits Capetown without calling at Constantia and going over the cellars of the Van Beenans and Cloetes. The stranger will find it difficult to believe that the choice wines which are presented to him are of colonial manufacture. The prices are most moderate and the flavor delicious. The variety of wines manufactured is very large. There are hock, sherry, port, Burgundy, and various other wines, while, on the other hand, the Cape brandy, which is manufactured in immense quantities, is as nauseous as can be well conceived. It is, however, universally drunk among the agriculturists and large numbers of other colonists. Constantia, however, is only a very small part of the wine-producing country. In the valleys and plains up to fifty miles away from Capetown there are vineyards and wine farms. In the midst of them we have villages—they could almost be called towns considering their populations—such as Paarl, Wellington, Hellenbosch, Somerset West, and other places. They are reached by a line of railway from Capetown, and this is the longest line of railway in the colony (there are no lines in the colony but those in the neighborhood of Capetown), extending, as it does, to Wellington, a distance of fifty-two miles. In these localities, in addition to the vinelands, considerable quantities of excellent grain are produced.

I will, just before leaving Capetown and neighborhood, point out that in one of the nooks of False Bay is Simon's Bay, the most perfectly-sheltered bay in the colony. Simon's Bay is the Cape naval station, and is about twenty-three miles from Capetown and eleven miles from Cape Point. The town is a small one. There is a patent slip, and vessels are easily supplied from the well-stocked stores of the town. The harbor arrangements of Capetown are such that passengers have every facility for landing, and there is a first-class transport service between Capetown and the diamond fields. The horse wagons of the Transfer Company are large, comfortable, and roomy. They carry twelve passengers and are dispatched once a week each way. The distance is, as I have already stated, over 700 miles, but the journey is accomplished in nine days by these wagons, which keep their time very punctually; all who have traveled by them speak in the highest terms of this mode of conveyance. There is nothing like it elsewhere in this colony or Natal. The journey is so arranged that persons are allowed certain hours for sleep and meals at the various hotels along the road, and the Company, to prevent passengers being imposed upon, have a regular scale of charge with the hotel keepers. The fare by the wagons is £12 for the whole journey. Those who do not care about being a little longer on the road can avail themselves of other conveyances. Messrs. Steytler & Steytler take passengers through for £10 by bullock wagon, and this charge includes provisions for the road. This firm also dispatches express carts, and have wagons engaged in carrying goods. In fact, the digger will find at Capetown every facility for his conveyance to the diamond fields, and in no other part of the colony is there a regular system of transport. The road throughout is a good one, as a proof of which I may mention that his Excellency Sir P. E. Wodehouse, the late governor of the colony, traversed the road between Wellington and the Orange River in an American spider, occupying only a period of eight days.

CHAPTER XIV

Port Elizabeth, about 500 miles from Capetown, on the Indian Ocean, has a population of over 12,000 inhabitants, about three-fourths of whom are European. The town is built principally under a bluff, and one long street running parallel with the shore, two miles in length, contains all the business houses, hotels, some residences, and churches. On the top of this bluff are most of the private residences, some churches, a fine botanical garden and hotel. The houses are principally built of brick and stone; very few wooden struc-

PORT ELIZABETH.

tures, on account of the scarcity of that article. Some of the buildings, such as the Town Hall, Custom House, Grey Institute, and several of the stores, would grace any city in the world. There is a much larger business carried on at Port Elizabeth than at Capetown. Their advantageous geographical position enables them to control all the interior trade of the eastern province of the Colony even as far as the Free State. The principal shipments are wool, of which Port Elizabeth shipped over 40,000,000 pounds in 1870. Algoa Bay, upon which Port Elizabeth is situated, is not much better than an open roadstead, and during the prevalence of certain winds it is quite dangerous, if vessels do not drop both their anchors and be ready to sail at a moment's notice. Most of the year, however, the harbor is quite safe, and they are building a wharf now that will facilitate the landing of cargo and passengers, which at present has to be done by surf boats. The merchants of Port Elizabeth have shown more enterprise than those of Capetown generally, but they have not yet started a transport company to the mines, but will probably do so soon.

The distance to Pniel *via* Craddock, Colesburg, and Jacobsdahl is 428 miles. There are two first-class hotels at Elizabeth, that charge 10s. per day, and about five second and third class, that charge from 4s. to 7s. for board and lodging. There are several boarding-houses, also, that charge about £5 a month for regular boarders. At the Town Hall there is a fine library, which is free to strangers. There are generally about twenty ships, steamers, barks, brigs, and schooners in the harbor, bound for England principally, and coastwise. Messrs. Taylor, Kemp & Co., American merchants, run a line of clippers from this place to Boston; and once in a while some other firms load a vessel with wool and skins, and send her to Boston or New York.

From Port Elizabeth to Pniel the roads were naturally good, and they are being improved every day. At most of the rivers there are fine iron or stone bridges built, and where there are none, there are large wagon ponts or ferries. On the Orange River, on this route, a bridge will shortly be built that will enable wagons to cross that stream at all seasons of the year. During the rainy season, wagons are frequently delayed for days at swollen streams, that at other seasons of the year are perfectly dry. It would not pay to have either a pont or bridge at these places at present.

The shortest route to the diamond fields from Port Elizabeth is *via* Craddock, Colesburg, Faursmith, and Jacobsdahl to Pniel. A post-cart runs all the way from Port Elizabeth to Pniel twice a week; but it runs day and night, and the carts are generally uncovered, or open and uncomfortable. But very few persons can stand the trip at once, and have to lie over half way, and run the risk of getting a seat in the next post-cart. There are plenty of ox teams going up from Port Elizabeth, but it takes them about twenty days at the best of seasons to make the trip. It is pretty certain that a transport company will be started to carry passengers with rapidity and comfort to the diamond mines. The duties on arms and ammunition are the same as at Capetown, viz., £1 a barrel for the gun, 6*d*. per lb. for powder, and 10 per cent. *ad valorem* on caps and lead; cartridges at the same ratio. There are duties on all other articles that are brought from foreign countries, excepting personal property.

Durbau, Port Natal, is 500 miles to the eastward of Port Elizabeth, and is a very pretty and substantially-built town of about 3,500 inhabitants, chiefly European. Port Natal, the harbor, is nearly land-locked, and is one of the most picturesque harbors in South Africa, and would be one of the best if the bar at the entrance was not so changeable. Sometimes there are ten and sometimes twenty feet of water on this bar. A contractor undertook to build a breakwater on the opposite side of the entrance to the city, from a bluff that rises to the height of 200 feet. It was built out several hundred yards, when it was found that it was on the wrong side of the entrance. It had then cost £60,000, and was doing more harm than good. Now they have started a pier from the other side, which may prove successful. In the meantime, large vessels have to remain outside, and unload and load by means of lighters. There are generally from ten to twenty vessels in the harbor. The port is about three miles from Durbau, and is connected with it by a railroad, the cars of which run every hour. This railroad has been extended to the River Umgani, three miles off, where the quarries are from which the stone is taken to build the pier or breakwater with. Durban is situated on the borders of the bay, on a sandy plain that extends from the seashore six miles to a line of hills called the Berea, which run parallel with the coast. The surrounding country is thickly filled with a large underbrush and small thorn trees. The city and Berea are connected by a fine macadamized road of four miles, made at a cost of £20,000. The main street of Durban, however, is not paved, and it is not unusual to see ox wagons stick in the sand, and they have to be partly unloaded before they can be moved, or else to hitch on another team of sixteen oxen (making thirty-two in all) to extricate it.

On the Berea most of the merchants reside, some of whom have very fine residences on its slopes, surrounded by luxuriant vegetation, including all kinds of tropical fruits and flowers. The climate is fine and particularly healthy. The main street of Durban presents a very fine appearance; the houses are chiefly built of brick or stone. There are at least a dozen hotels, that charge from 4s. to 10s. per day. The post-cart runs every day to Pietermaritzburg, sixty miles inland, carrying passengers. Pietermaritzburg is the capital of the Colony of Natal, and contains about 3,500 inhabitants. It is called a city, because the Bishop of the Church of England (Bishop Colenso) resides there. There are some very fine buildings in Pietermaritzburg, and the new State House would be an ornament to any city in the world. This is the seat of government, which is represented by a Lieutenant-Governor and his Cabinet, appointed by the Crown, and the Legislative Assembly, elected by the colonists. There are about 17,000 white people in Natal, and the area of the colony is about 17,000 square miles. It abounds in rivers, which run from the Drakenburg mountains to the sea, a distance generally of about 200 miles. These mountains rise to an elevation of 6,000 feet, and are frequently snow-clad. There is a gradual slope to the sea-coast. On these slopes are grown corn, cotton, wheat, rye, oats, apples, peaches, plums, and melons. Along the coast, and as far back as say twenty miles, coffee and sugar are grown to a great extent; also oranges, bananas, and pineapples. American emigration is sought for, and Americans are treated with consideration and kindness. There are several transport wagons running from Pietermaritzburg to the diamond fields. The roads are naturally fine, and if miners desire to purchase their own team, they can always find plenty of oxen and wagons on the market square on Saturdays, or they can have a wagon made to suit them by one of the several wagon-makers, or they can purchase their oxen or mules from the surrounding farmers. Oxen are sold at £4 a head, and mules and horses from £8 to £10 a head. Large wagons with covers are from £80 to £100 each. It is necessary to have at least fourteen oxen; most wagons have sixteen. Spring wagons, to be drawn by six or eight mules, are made for £80. At the auction sales, second-hand wagons are frequently sold for half the above prices. Everything else that a miner requires can be purchased at Durban or Pietermaritzburg. The duty on firearms is 10s. a barrel, and on cartridges the same as at Capetown and Port Elizabeth. Gunpowder is not allowed to be imported except by the Government, from whom it can be purchased. One thousand cartridges are allowed to be brought in for each breech-loader that is imported; of course, duty is charged.

A route to the diamond fields will soon be opened from another sea-port (Delagoa Bay), described in another chapter. It is also the nearest port to the gold mines of the Limpopo and Zambesi Rivers and their tributaries.

CHAPTER XV.

There are several ways of getting to the above South African ports from America. Isaac Taylor & Co., No. 8 Kilby Street, Boston, and No. 40 Broadway, New York, have a line of vessels running to Port Elizabeth to their branch house there (Messrs. Taylor, Kemp & Co.) Sometimes they send their vessels to Capetown to Messrs. G. S. Holmes & Co., American merchants. Both of the above firms are in first-class standing, and the members of the firms are genial and kind-hearted gentlemen, and always glad to see Americans and forward their interests. Most vessels for South African ports are despatched from Boston, some from New York, and a few from Baltimore. Pickering, Winslow & Co., of Boston, frequently load a vessel for South Africa; Messrs. S. L. Merchant & Co., shipping merchants at New York, Boston and Baltimore, are always posted about the sailing of African vessels, and will gladly furnish any information in their power to intending emigrants. The passage to any of the above ports in Africa is generally made in about sixty or seventy days, and the fare, first-class, is £30, and second-class £20; most of the vessels from America have good cabins and give good fare. There are two small steamers running from Capetown to Natal, stopping at Algoa Bay, Port Elizabeth. The fare to Port Elizabeth on these steamers is £6 6s., and through to Natal £10. Second-class is about two-thirds of the above fare.

Another way to get to Africa is to go by way of England; the passage to England by steamer is made in from ten to fifteen days, and the fare, first-class, ranges from £15 to £25, and second or steerage from £6 to £10. On the sailing vessels the fare is much lower, and it takes from fifteen to thirty days to make the passage. At Liverpool, most all the Americans stop at the Washington Hotel, just opposite the London railway station; the charge is about 10s. per day. There are other hotels that range from 4s. to 6s. a day for board and lodging.

If, in the event of a vessel not being up for South Africa at Liverpool, parties can always be sure of finding at least half a dozen up at London. The fare from Liverpool to London is, first-class, 30s., second, 20s., and third, about 10s.; it is two hundred miles and is made in less than five hours. Board can be obtained in London at from 4s. to 20s. a day, the latter at the Charing Cross and Langham Hotels at the West End, and the former in the city, near the Bank of England. There are two good hotels that I have tried in the city, and where a great many Americans, chiefly business men, stop at; one is the Cathedral Hotel, St. Paul's Churchyard, and the other is Faul's Hotel, No. 7 King Street, Cheapside; the charge at this latter hotel is from 2s. to 5s. a night for a room; 2s. for breakfast and 2s. for dinner if you dine at the house, or you can dine at the numerous restaurants that are to be found throughout London. Faul's Hotel is convenient to the Bank of England and the business houses of the city, from where the different outfits are to be purchased. There are two regular lines of steamers from England to South Africa. The Union Line carry the royal mails, and leave Plymouth on the 10th and 25th of each month, carrying passengers to Capetown and Port Elizabeth, and forward them by small steamers to Port Natal. The office is No. 3 East India Chambers, Leadenhall Street, London, where tickets can be purchased, including railway fare from London to Plymouth; it takes about thirty-two days to make the run to Capetown, where they remain a few days, and then go on to Port Elizabeth (in about forty-eight hours), where they reship to Port Natal. First-class fare from England to Capetown is usually £42, second-class fare is £30. The fares are lower than that, when there are any opposition steamers on the route, and that leave about the same time that they do; this line set a good table, and have excellent sleeping accommodation.

The Good Hope Line have about five steamers now, and leave Victoria Docks, London, about once a month, for Capetown, Algoa Bay, and through to Natal; their vessels are large, and give very good food, and have good sleeping accommodation. They take about thirty-five days to Capetown, and their fare is about £5 less than the Union Line for each class. Their office is at No. 117 Leadenhall Street, London. Once in a while there are outside steamers put up for South Africa, which charge still less than the above lines. There are at least half a dozen lines of clippers that run to the different South African ports from London : among them the Aberdeen Line, one of whose vessels leaves St. Katherine's Dock, London, for Natal once a month, and they make their passage in from sixty to eighty days. They charge £30 first-class fare, and £16 second-class or steerage ; the latter have to find their own bedding, and it is advisable for them to take a few extra stores, such as captain's biscuits, preserved salmon and sardines, ground coffee, sugar, and some preserved fruits. Some of the other lines run only to Capetown and Port Elizabeth, and the fare is the same to each of these ports as to Natal.

CHAPTER XVI

The Bay of Lorenzo Marquez, or Delagoa Bay, is situated in lat. 26° S. and long. 32° 40″ E. The town of the same name is one and a-half miles long and a quarter of a mile broad, containing 37 houses with flat roofs and 127 thatched ones. The population numbers 192 whites and 775 colored people.

The harbor is five miles long and three and a-half miles broad in its broadest place. There are two channels in it, called North and South. The southern channel is accessible to vessels of the largest tonnage; small vessels may tack about in any part of the harbor.

The natural beauty of Lorenzo Marquez can hardly be described ; and, regarding the safety of vessels, easy entrance to the bay and anchorage, the harbor is superior to all others of South Africa.

The following is a guide to vessels entering the bay : when approaching Injak Island, coming from south, avoid the sandbanks near that island; take Point Vermilion during day time, and run along the channel marked in the map; avoid coming too near Sheffina Island on account of the sandbanks, which stretch some distance into the bay; when arrived at two and a-half miles from Point Vermilion, keep to the southwest, and afterward right on toward the anchorage, which is just in front of the town.

The greater part of the present trade is with the natives, bringing ivory, ostrich feathers, rhinoceros horns, hippopotamus teeth, wax, urzella, etc., for sale or barter. The Portuguese Government intend to reopen the roads to the Transvaal immediately, to bring thereby the Vaal River diamond fields, the Tati gold fields, and the considerable Transvaal produce within easy reach. Lorenzo Marquez, will, without doubt, become, within a short period, the key to the rich mines and products of interior Africa. See routes laid down on map.

The bay abounds with whales, the rivers with hippopotami (sea cows) ; the soil of the district is very fertile, and fit for the cultivation of coffee, cotton, rice, tobacco, indigo—in fact, for all that the Old and New Worlds produce.

In the map the gold region is laid down, though it has always been known that it exists in these parts, besides copper, iron, and coal; the exact spot has only lately been discovered, and it requires only enterprise to enrich people and country.

Five rivers run into the bay, of which two, *i. e.*, Uzutu and Manissa, are to some extent navigable.

The climate on the immediate coast is healthy, with the exception of three months in the year, namely, January, February, and March, when it happens that some of the inhabitants get low fever ; but since the same takes place in Natal, and that is considered healthy, it is not worth taking notice of, and only one or two miles from the coast, the climate is excellent. The lands in the district are well watered and wooded, the wood being of valuable kinds.

A Mr. McCorkandale, who has been the President of the Transvaal Republic's right-hand man, and who is the only live man that I have seen in South Africa, has been to England to try and procure a sea-port on Injack Island for the Transvaal Republic, that the British Government have taken possession of. I learn that he has succeeded in gaining the consent of the Government, and has been trying to raise capital to open the port and the river. This river, with a little dredging, can be opened as far as the Bembo Mountains, so that a Mississippi-built steamer could run thus far at all seasons of the year. At the foot of the mountains, on the highlands, he proposes to start a town that will be in a healthy location. It is about six hours' run from the island to this location, and could be run at all seasons without danger of catching the fever among the swamps. From McCorkandale's proposed town a road will run in a northwest direction to New Scotland, among the Drakenburgs, and from thence branch off north and south into the interior of the Transvaal Republic. New Scotland is already settled, and quite a number of farms are under successful cultivation. There are also several stores in the district; and now, if McCorkandale succeeds in getting up this sea-port and line of steamboats, an immense trade will spring up with the interior and foreign countries, and all the Transvaalers would ship their wool by this route. It is obvious what importance is in store for the Bay of Lorenzo Marquez. Coal and gold fields lay in easy distance; and should the latter prove to extend their auriferous stratas as far as Lobombo, perhaps (interrupted by this volcanic mountain range) somewhat farther toward south-east, and should the River Manissa prove navigable as high up as the sharp bend toward southwest, the distance would be reduced to an insignificant minimum. Besides, the district Lydemburg is not at all poorly provided with other useful minerals, as copper, iron, and, very probably, lead. Should the climate of the immediate coast be considered too unhealthy, however, it is no more so than Natal. Very soon an elevated tract of land near Lobombo will be reached in less than two days. A railroad might be constructed over the well-wooded country, following the strike of the auriferous rocks toward the north-west, as far as Tati gold fields, being 370 miles (Engl. naut.) distant in a straight line from Lorenzo Marquez. No mountain range would be in the way for the construction of this railroad.

Proposal of law published according to Article 12 of the fundamental law, and according to Article 16 of resolution of the Volksraad, dated 21st December,. 1870 :

Whereas it has been found necessary to make such regulations that the first discoverer of gold fields in the South African Republic shall be entitled to reward, the following is hereby enacted :

ART. 1.—*Bona fide* finders of gold in this Republic must make such discovery known, and prove it by producing a sample of not less than two ounces in weight of the gold to the magistrate, or any other, for the occasion nominated, qualified official in the district where the gold has been found; and have to request that a piece of ground of ten miles square be marked out, whose middle point must be the place or spot where the gold was found, and which request has to be registered.

ART. 2.—To the discoverer of a gold-bearing quartz reef, on Government ground or uninspected grounds, within the limits of this State, shall be granted right for a certain time to search on half a mile square; and in case alluvial gold is found, the discoverer has a right to a quarter mile square.. Both may afterward form the middle point of gold fields of ten miles square.

ART. 3.—The State's President shall, after satisfactory proof of beforementioned discovery has been produced, grant a miner's right for twelve months.

ART. 4.—When the miner's right, mentioned in foregoing article, has expired, the miner or discoverer can select a further exploration right of 600 by 750 feet, from a quartz reef or alluvial gold ground, and the continual exploration right of 250 feet square, both subject to regulations to be made hereafter.

ART. 5.—On a gold field where there exists a continued exploration right, only a further right for search for a certain time can be granted.

ART. 6.—When a gold field of ten miles square has been marked out, every one who wishes to dig for gold must provide himself with a miner's license.

ART. 7.—Proprietors of private property on which gold is found have the right to mine for gold without license on their own grounds, and have the right to prevent others to dig for gold on their lands.

ART. 8.—For a miner's license shall be paid one pound sterling, and be in force during one year.

ART. 9.—An official appointed by Government shall mark out the ground and place the beacons.

ART. 10.—The Executive Council shall from time to time frame further regulations upon this subject.

ART. 11.—Any person, with the exception of proprietors of goldbearing ground, who shall be found gold-digging without license, or refuses to present his license to the appointed official when requested to do so, shall be punished with money fine or imprisonment.

ART. 12.—The export duty on gold shall hereafter be regulated.

FORM OF LICENSE.

No....   Date....................

License is hereby granted to   to dig and search for gold on government ground on the gold fields situated in the district   pointed out by authorized Government official, and on private property, with the permission of the proprietor.

This license is in force during one year, and has to be presented upon request to the authorized official.   Signature...............

TABLE OF REWARD.

£500 for discovery of a gold field which yields 500 ounces of gold a month during twelve months.

£750 for discovery of a gold field which yields from 500 to 1,000 ounces as above.

£1,000 for discovery of a gold field which yields 1,000 ounces or more, as above.

Art. 13. This law shall be in force according to Art. 69 of the fundamental law.

Government's Office, Pretoria, 30*th January*, 1871.
(Per order.)
B. C. E. Proes, *Government Secretary*.

CHAPTER XVII.
THE GREAT DIAMONDS OF THE WORLD AND THEIR LEGENDS.

How much romance is connected with the bright, invincible, nonpareil adamant, the most refulgent and the most precious of gems—the diamond! And yet it consists solely of the elementary substance, carbon, crystallized and in its greatest purity. Although it can not be electrified by heat, it becomes electric by friction. Its specific gravity is about 3.6. Its crystals have often curvilinear faces and edges, but its primary form is a regular octahedron. Its lamellar structure and peculiar conformation, together with its weight, form the chief means of distinguishing it from the many stones which at first sight appear similar. The diamond is the king of the mineral kingdom, while rubies, sapphires, *et hoc genus*, form only the aristocracy. A few of the nobility and many of the plebeian orders seem to claim relationship with the monarch; but however plausible the pretensions of a topaz or a rock crystal may seem at first sight, when weighed in the balance they are found wanting. Many people imagine that diamonds ought to be colorless like water; but although they are commonly so, yet from a foreign intermixture they are sometimes white, green, yellow, gray, brown, and more rarely red, black, orange, and blue. Real gems have often been mistaken for

"Faux brillians, et morceaux de verre,"

and there are extraordinary tales on record of diamonds

whose value has been unrecognized. The thieves who stole the Countess of Ellesmere's jewels, finding the gems carelessly wrapped up, imagined that the very finest stones were mere glass ornaments "worn by player folks," and the Jew to whom they were offered for sale was of the same opinion. The great Sanci diamond, worn at the battle of Nancy by Charles the Bold of Burgundy, was picked up on the field by a Swiss mercenary, who sold it for 1s. 8d. to a priest, and the latter, in his turn, disposed of it for 2s. 6d. Similar stories are told of other great diamonds, and even at the present day it is frequently found no easy task to distinguish a real brilliant from an imitation. In the beginning of 1854, an English gentleman was robbed of seven brilliants, and advertised them in the *Times*, besides leaving no other means of discovery untried. He heard nothing of them till the following February, when they were returned to him by a clerk who had bought a tin box containing them for a pot of beer. He had worn the finest for months in a scarf-pin, and the jeweler who set it, as well as his friends and himself, were under the impression that it was only a "pretty bit of glass."

But books could be filled with anecdotes about diamonds and romances have been connected with them from the time when their possession first began to create envy and bloodshed in India until a revolution was hastened in France by the famous diamond necklace of Marie Antoinette. Space will only permit us to pass in review before our readers some of the greatest diamonds of the world, and their legends, and then it will be desirable to refer to the regions where they are found, with the view of proving that the geology of South Africa is similar to that of other countries where gold and diamonds exist.* The history of their discovery in South Africa will follow, and we hope to give some interesting information regarding the Cape of Good Hope Fields and the gems that have been found on them, as well as to place before our readers reliable information regarding

---

* Mr. Emmanuel is forced publicly to admit that diamonds have been found in South Africa, but couples the tardy acknowledgment with an absurd statement (probably based upon Mr. Gregory's information) that the country in which they are found is not geologically "diamondiferous."

their value and the means of ascertaining their identity. It is well known that the largest reputed diamond in the world was found in Brazil, and belongs to the House of Braganza. It weighs 1,680* carats (nearly eleven ounces), and was found in 1808 by a negro, who was wise enough to solicit a personal interview with Don John of Portugal. The issue of this was that the Regent granted him an escort, under which the negro shortly returned, bringing the great diamond, which looked like a darkish yellow pebble, kidney-shaped, and oblong—about the size of a pullet's egg. The Brazilian jewelers valued it at three hundred million pounds sterling, and advised its being left rough and unpolished. The finder obtained his liberty and a pension. There are doubts as to whether or not this gem is really a diamond, and it is suspected that it may be only a colorless topaz.

The Koh-i-noor (Mountain of Light), was originally an immense diamond weighing 793 carats, and was a source of war and misfortune in India for more than a thousand years. According to Hindoo tradition, it was found in a Golconda mine, and first belonged to the god "Krischnu," from whose idol it was stolen by a wild Delhi chief, who wore it ostentatiously in his hat. From this spoiler Ala el Din seized the prey, and eventually, in 1526, the diamond came into the possession of the Moguls. The great Aurungzebe resolved to have it polished, but this task was very unskillfully performed. According to Dr. Behe (paper read before the British Association, 1851), "There was found at the capture of Coochan, among the jewels of the harem of Reeza Kooli Khan, a large diamond slab, supposed to have been broken from one side of the Koh-i-noor. It weighed about 130 carats, and one part of its superfices corresponded exactly with one side of the Koh-i-noor." After the Koh-i-noor had belonged successively to the Bahmani, Khilji, Lodi, and Mogul kings, it came, in 1739, into the hands of Nadir Shah, who called it by its present name. From him it went into the possession of the Abdali monarchs of Afghanistan, the last of whom (Shah Sujah) was forced to present it to Runjeet Singh, the

---

* Emmannel, in his work on diamonds, says that it weighs 1,880 carats, but all the other authorities consulted state the weight given in the text.

Lion of the Punjaub. On the annexation of this territory and the abdication of the Maharajah Dhuleep Singh in 1849, it became the property of Queen Victoria, and the principal crown jewel of the British Empire. The farther this stone was cut into the harder it seemed to be, and thirty-five days were devoted to the operation. It is now a beautiful rose-cut brilliant weighing $106\frac{1}{16}$ carats, valued at £120,664.

In the year 1760 a diamond weighing 367 carats was found at Landak, in the Island of Borneo. The news of its discovery was the signal for a war furiously waged for upward of twenty years between two of the native tribes. Eventually the diamond remained in the possession of its first owner, the Rajah of Mattam, who so superstitiously believed that the fortunes of his house depended upon its possession, that he refused to sell it to the Dutch for a couple of gun-boats and a quarter million of dollars in specie. The Orloff diamond ($194\frac{1}{4}$ carats), which belongs to the Russian Crown, was found by an Indian, who made it form the eye of a popular idol. It is said that a Frenchman who coveted this valuable optic became a pagan priest, and thus gained the opportunity of stealing it. He then sold it in Malabar for £2,800. After many adventures it was purchased in 1775 by the Empress Catharine of Russia from the Armenian Schaffras for £90,000 in cash, an annuity of £4,000, and a patent of nobility. It is now placed in the Imperial scepter of Russia. The Pitt diamond, found in India ($136\frac{3}{4}$ carats), belonged to the French Crown, and was worn by the Empress Eugenie at her marriage. The Right Hon. William Pitt, Governor of Fort St. George, purchased it for £12,500, and it was sold to the Regent Duke of Orleans in 1717 for £135,000, while in 1791 a commission of jewelers valued it at £500,000. Louis the Sixteenth wore it in his hat at his coronation, and Napoleon the First fixed it in the pommel of his sword. At the battle of Waterloo it was seized by the Prussians.

The Star of the South, which weighed in the rough 254 carats, was found by a negro in Brazil in 1853. It was reduced by cutting to 125 carats, and belongs to the famous diamond-cutter, Costar, of Amsterdam. The Maximilian

SOUTH AFRICAN DIAMOND FIELDS.

diamond, owned by the Austrian Royal Family, is of a yellow color, and rose cut. It was originally in the hands of the Medici, and came to its present owners through the Grand Duke of Tuscany. It weighs 139½ carats, and is valued at £155,682.

No gem is more pure or owns a more romantic legend than the Sanci diamond (almond shape, weight 53½ carats), which originally belonged to an Eastern merchant, who sold it to Charles the Bold of Burgundy. After his death, at the battle of Nancy, in 1475, it was picked up on the field and sold first for 1s. 8d. and then for half-a crown. After this, it passed through a number of adventures, till it came into the possession of Antonio, King of Portugal. It was first pledged to a French gentleman, named De Sanci, for 40,000 francs, and subsequently sold to him for one hundred thousand. A descendant of this man confided it to the care of a servant, who mysteriously disappeared; but his master was confident that he had been faithful, and caused a strict search to be made, which resulted in the diamond being found in the stomach of the murdered man. The Baron de Sanci afterward disposed of this jewel to James the Second, and it was sold to the French Court by that monarch for £25,000. It was subsequently in the possession of the Spanish Prince of Peace, Godoy, and was sold by him to Prince Demidoff. It was recently purchased by Sir Jamsetjee Jejeebhoy for £20,000.

The Imperial Family of Russia not only owns the Orloff diamond, but one which has been valued at £369,800. Holland possesses a modest conical-shaped gem worth £10,368. But the Persian Court outshines most European ones in its display of jewelry. Two celebrated stones owned by the Shah are the "Sea of Glory," and the "Mountain of Light," valued at £145,000 and £34,848 respectively. The Pigott diamond was brought to England by Earl Pigott, Governor-General of India, weighs 82¼ carats, and was disposed of by lottery for £30,000. It was subsequently bought by Rundell and Bridge for £6,000, and sold by them to the Pasha of Egypt for £30,000. A beautiful green diamond weighing 48½ carats, is to be seen at Dresden, and there is a fine red diamond of 10 carats which cost the

Emperor Paul of Russia 100,000 roubles. A London merchant named Dresden* owned a beautiful drop-shaped brilliant weighing 76½ carats; and one of the marriage presents made by Napoleon the Third to Eugenie was a magnificent brilliant weighing 51 carats. The Nassak diamond (78⅝ carats) was taken by the Marquis of Hastings at the conquest of the Deccan, and is now owned by the Marquis of Westminster.

The celebrated diamond known as "The Hope" is of a most brilliant sapphire blue color, weighs 44½ carats, and was exhibited in London during 1851. For a gem of the same hue, weighing 29½ carats, George the Fourth paid £22,000. The former of these blue diamonds was owned by the late eccentric and celebrated Philip Hope, Esq., whose wonderful collection of precious stones was a fine gathering of specimens in various states and of different colors. In order to show what great varieties of diamonds exist, it is only necessary to catalogue this collection. In it there were brilliants jet black, very fine topaz color, besides some of the deepest ruby pallais hue, lemon, cymophane (green and orange), chrysolite, beautiful light green, aquamarine (sea green), deep sapphire blue, light blue, milky blue, deep orange, brown, dusky red, deep garnet, jacinth (tawny red), and rose color. All of these stones of so many hues were veritable diamonds, and most of them passed into the hands of the well-known English firm of Hunt and Roskell, who showed them to the world at the Great Exhibition of 1851.

COUNTRIES IN WHICH DIAMONDS ARE FOUND.—THEIR GEOLOGY.—DIAMOND WASHING.

Diamonds are found in Hindostan, Borneo, Sumatra, Brazil, the Ural Mountains, Australia, and South Africa.† If we can believe what is recorded on the subject, India formerly produced an immense number. Tavernier, a French jeweler,

---

* This gem was recently in the possession of a Parsee, who sold it to an Indian Prince.

† They are said also to have been found in North America. There seems little doubt that small ones have been picked up in California.

who traveled in the East about the middle of the seventeenth century, mentions that in his time the mines of Golconda employed 60,000 persons. Fareehta, the historian, asserts that the Sultan Mahmoud (1177–1206) left at his death more than 400 pounds weight of diamonds. If these statements be even approximately correct, the diamond mines of Hindostan are now comparatively exhausted. At the present day, the principal are at Sumbhulpore, where the business is hereditary in two tribes, supposed to be descendants of slaves imported for the purpose. They number between 400 and 500 persons, possess sixteen villages, and work during the dry season in the bed of the Mahanuddy, from Kinderpore to Sinepore. Although Golconda has been always famous for its diamonds, the fact is that they were merely polished there, being generally found at Parteall, near the southern frontier of the Nizam's dominions. This extensive territory lies to the north-west of the Presidency of Madras, and its principal river is the Godavery, with numerous tributaries. The metamorphic rocks of the Eastern and Western Ghauts continue to the north of the Godavery, and the triangular region inclosed between these great mountain ranges and that river is principally covered with trappean rocks, although scattered portions of secondary and tertiary strata are to be found.* A distinguished traveler (M. Voysey), in his "Asiatic Researches," states, that at one place where diamonds were found, he particularly noticed a range of hills, named the Nalla Malla, or Blue Mountains, composed of schistose rocks of all varieties, from clay slate to pure limestone, accompanied with quartz rock sandstone, sandstone brescia, flinty slate, and a tuffaceous limestone containing embedded, rounded, and angular masses of all these rocks. "These are bounded on all sides by granite, which appears to pass under and form the base. The only rock of this formation on which the diamond is found is the sandstone brescia."

The physical conformation of Borneo and Sumatra is sim-

---

* Eight or nine years ago, geological surveyors under Professor Oldham, were appointed, and by means of their labors a great deal of information has been obtained; but only the general features of the geological structure of India are yet known.

ilar. In the latter island the mountain systems are of trachyte, granite, limestone, red sandstone, and a wide-spread conglomerate composed of granitic and quartzose particles, the hollows in many places being filled with lava. In the valleys tertiary deposits are found. Gold is widely diffused; and here it seems desirable to call the reader's special attention to the fact, *that in every country where diamonds are found, gold has also been discovered in large quantities.* Dr. Gardner* found gold mines in existence within the diamond regions of Brazil, and speaks of "a vein proceeding downward through a soft, white, arenacious, schistose rock. I found them occupied in washing the material they had taken out, which proved to be very uncertain in its product, some days yielding one, two, and three ounces of gold." From the Ural Mountains, in the year 1862, no less than 6,660 English lbs. of gold were extracted. The heaviest nugget found weighed 80 lbs. This chain is composed principally of crystalline and metamorphic rocks, granite, porphyry, gneiss, chloritic and micaceous schists. Humboldt foretold that diamonds would be discovered here, and his prophecy has been fulfilled. Besides these there are large and beautiful emeralds, as well as the beryl, topaz, and amethyst.† It is well known that when, in 1846, Count Strelecki submitted to Sir Roderick Murchison a series of Australian rock and mineral specimens, that experienced geologist recognized in them such a remarkable resemblance to the auriferous rocks of the Ural Mountains as to make him positive that the precious metal would be found in large quantities within Australia.

In that vast island an immense central expanse of tertiary beds is surrounded by a continuous belt of plutonic and metamorphic rocks. Numerous and often extensive patches of igneous rocks are found through primary, secondary, or tertiary strata, and a broad strip of palæozoic rocks extends from the shore of the Gulf of Carpentaria to Bass's Straits.

---

* "Travels in the Interior of Brazil, principally through the Northern Provinces and the Gold and Diamond Districts." By George Gardner, M.D., F.L.S. Second edition.

† Some emeralds found on the eastern slope, in the district of Ekatermburg, weigh 13 dwts. 9 grains.

There can be no doubt about the similarity of the geology of the auriferous regions of Australia to those of South-Eastern Africa, and in the sequel it will be shown that, so far from our own diamond and gold fields presenting any exception to geological rules, they are merely additional instances of their accuracy. In Brazil, diamonds are usually found in dilluvial, gravelly soil, but Dr. Gardner (page 346) states positively, "That is not, however, the matrix in which they have originally been formed. Whatever may be the case in other countries, I remain perfectly satisfied that here they have originally been formed in the metamorphic quarto-schistose rock, of which the mountains in the diamond district are constituted, and that they have, during a long series of years, been washed down along with the other débris." These metamorphic rocks being rather soft, are easily disintegrated, and small masses have frequently been found containing diamonds embedded in them. In Brazil, when the diamond formation consists of loose gravel, it is called "cascalho," and when of ferruginous conglomerate, it is named "canga." Diamonds are generally found in an agglomerate of rounded pebbles and sand, formed by the decomposition of granite and mica slate. The bed varies from one to four feet in thickness. The "cascalho" generally rests upon a substratum of hard clay, beneath which are found the solid chistose rocks which generally prevail throughout the diamond district. Sometimes "canga" rests upon a kind of limestone, in which case it is always found to be rich in diamonds.

The following is the manner in which washing is carried on: along one side of a pond of water a range of troughs is placed, whose sides next the water are low. Into each trough gravel is placed, on which water is immediately dashed with great force. By this means, and stirring at frequent intervals with a small kind of hoe, it is freed from earth and sand, when the larger particles of gravel are taken out, and any large diamonds are found. The labor is continued from morning until four o'clock in the afternoon, when the "cascalho," now cleansed and purified, is carried to the side of a little stream of running water to be finally washed. At this operation each man has a large, flat, wooden vessel, which he uses for washing out the gravel. This is called a batcia, and in the bottom of it is always found a small quantity of gold dust, which is carefully preserved.* It is specially worthy of note that it has been satisfactorily proved, by means of specimens sent to the Royal Society of Edinburgh, that the Brazil diamond deposits are exactly similar to some of those in Hindostan, situate in a quartzose mica slate, or itacalumite.

Since Dr. Gardner visited Brazil in 1836, large additional fields have been discovered; and Captain Burton† mentions that the great Province of Bahia only commenced to work its Chapada or diamantine plateau in 1845-6, and now extends its wealth almost to the seaboard. The rivers Parahyba du Sul, Verde, and Tibagy, in the provinces of Sao Paulo and Parana, have produced diamonds; and "evidently Brazil has a vast extent of diamantine ground reserved for future generations to work with intelligence, and especially by means of machinery."‡ He says prospecting for diamonds is done as follows: "The vegetable humus, the underlying clay, and the desmonte or inundation sand are removed by the almocatre (an oval-shaped, blunt-headed iron), till the laborers reach the gem-bearing 'cascalho.' This first work is usually an open cut of a few feet square. The larger fragments of quartz are then removed by the hand, the gravel is washed in a bácco, canôa, or cuyaca, and finally the batcia is used." At the Jequitinhonha diamond diggings, Burton found a strong dyke of ashlar and earth run out from the right bank to the mid-stream of the Rio das Pedras, and machinery

---

* This privilege of diamond-washing has for many years ceased to be a Government monopoly in Brazil. One writer estimates that, "within the space of fourteen leagues square, it is beneath the mark to state that 10,000 individuals subsist entirely upon the product of diamonds and gold extracted from its soil. I was assured that the excitement produced by this kind of life is like that of a gambler—whoever enters upon it never renounces it."

† "Explorations of the Highlands of the Brazil, with a full account of the Gold and Diamond Mines." By Captain Richard F. Burton. 1869.

‡ In another place (vol. ii., p. 154) he remarks: "As yet the diamantine formations of the Brazil have been barely scratched, and the works have been compared with those of beavers. The rivers have not been turned; the deep pools above and below the rapids, where the great deposits must collect, have not been explored even with the diving helmet; the dry method of extraction, long ago known in Hindostan, is still here unknown." If Brazil has not been even scratched, what has been done to South Africa?

with water motive power at work. At the Canteiro mine, which had previously been given up as exhausted, £6,000 were spent by Sr. Vedigal before he got it into proper working order. During the season, three hundred slaves are employed, and the monthly expense is £750. When the rich cascalho or canga is struck, it is at once disposed in heaps near the lavadeiro or washing place, which is an open thatched ranch containing troughs, each four feet long, three feet broad, and one deep. The system of diamond-washing already described is copied from Hindostan, with a few improvements, such as the peneira, or sieve pan, fitted at the bottom with a piece of tin pierced with holes, averaging six to the inch, and arresting stones of half a carat. The most scrupulous care is taken that the smallest gems do not escape, and a good washer employs from half an hour to three-quarters of an hour to exhaust a single panfull. So absolutely necessary is washing considered to be, that where it is not possible, no attempt is made to find diamonds. The owners of mines suffer very heavily from constant thefts, and a receiver of stolen goods settles near every new digging as surely as a public-house follows a hydropathic establishment. In describing the Sao Joao mine, Burton says: "Through the ferruginous sandstone and the white felspathic matter run dykes and lines of fragmentary rock crystal. Large pieces of imperfect specular iron and thin strata of quartz, yellow and brown at the junction, thread the argile; and I was shown a specimen of fine sandy conglomerate, blackened and scarified by the injection of melted matter. Lieut.-Colonel Brant gave me a fragment of large-grained clay, reddish-colored with oxide, and showing a small brilliant imbedded in it." During the first twenty years of diamond discovery in Brazil, no less than 1,000 ounces of diamonds were annually obtained. Castelnau (vol. ii., p. 398) estimates the total value of the Minas Gerais exportation at 300,000,000 francs; and, coming down to recent times, it is stated in Mr. Nathar's annual report (Rio de Janeiro) that from 1861 to 1867, diamonds to the value of £1,888,000 have been sent out of the country.

A HINT TO MAKE MONEY AT THE DIAMOND FIELDS.

When I first went to the fields, over a year ago, there was a great scarcity of the proper kind of sieving-wire; most of the stuff sent there was either too small or too large in the mesh; or else the wire from which it was made was too fine, and would not last more than a month before breaking through. Once in a while a small lot of the right kind would arrive, which would be immediately bought up at an extravagant figure. Upon my arrival at the fields the second time, after an absence of seven months, and during my five months' stay there, no improvement had been made in this respect, although the merchants had known of the want of good sieving for over a year, but had not sent the proper order home to meet it; and consequently *good* sieving was to be had in very small quantities, and once in a while only, and even poor sieving was difficult to find. The kind of sieving needed there should be one-eighth of an inch mesh clear, and the wire should be No. 16, or the sixteenth of an inch in thickness. Now, the one-eighth inch mesh wil' allow two out of five half-carat diamonds to pass through, but not a three-quarter carat one; and it does not pay the miner to sort over the great amount of fine stuff that would accumulate if a finer mesh was used for saving a half-carat diamond. The time saved in not sorting this fine stuff could be more advantageously used in getting through a much larger quantity of coarse stuff, thereby coming to a larger diamond, and working out the claim quicker than otherwise—and time is *diamonds* there. Any one shipping a few thousand yards of the above-mentioned wire could dispose of it for at least a pound sterling a yard. The American Engine Company brought about fifty yards of this kind of wire from America, and when they were about to leave the fields they sold it for £2 a yard, and hundreds inquiring for more.

Another thing greatly needed at the mines is twenty-pound sledge-hammers, for breaking up the hard lumps that are taken out of the white strata at De Beer's New Rush; a few thousands of these would sell at a pound sterling each. While speaking of these hard lumps, I may as well mention that thousands of cart-loads are hauled out into the veld every week, and they, most undoubtedly, contain diamonds—and large ones too. Now, if any one has inventive genius enough to make a simple, cheap, and cheaply-working machine to crush these lumps—*without crushing the diamonds*—there is a larger fortune for him lying about loose in this veld than has ever been accumulated in South Africa by any one man. One of the most important drawbacks to living and mining at the dry diggings is the want of water. The dams supply water for the cattle, but is too impure for human beings, and the numerous wells do not supply a sufficient quantity for drinking. There are two ways of supplying this deficiency, one requiring at least £10,000 to be invested, and the other not more than £500, but not so sure as the first. The first would consist of a line of sheet-iron pipes running from the nearest fall or drift on the Vaal River, over hill and dale, to the highest point at or near Du Toit's Pan and De Beer's, which point is 130 feet higher than the Vaal River, and the distance is sixteen miles. A great many will think it absurd to lay a sheet-iron pipe, as they imagine that it will easily corrode and burst; but this is a mistake. A sheet-iron piping could be made, and has been made in Sweden and used in California, say eleven inches in diameter, and galvanized, that would stand a pressure of a column of water 350 feet high, and last for years. Through this piping water could be forced at the rate of say ten miles an hour, which would give as much water at the reservoir at Du Toit's Pan as could be floated in a four-foot canal at two miles an hour. The water would be forced through the piping by a hydraulic engine, worked by a French turbine water-wheel that could be set alongside of the Vaal River at the mouth of a four-foot race, with a fall of ten feet only. This motive power would not have need of much attention; one man could attend it. The piping could be laid on the surface, and when full of water, and the pressure on, an elephant could not make an impression upon it. Of course, it could be sunk or carried over the roads. From the reservoir the water could be led in all directions, by its own pressure, for miles and miles. The spot where I would propose to build the reservoir is the highest between the Vaal and Modder Rivers, and half-way between De Beer's and Du Toit's Pan (about three-quarters of a mile from each). An immense dividend could be made from this water by supplying the inhabitants with drinking and washing water at a penny a bucket. I have paid sixpence a bucket at the New Rush, and found it difficult to get it at that price. Now, there are say 25,000 people at the three camps—Du Toit's Pan, De Beer's, and the New Rush—and there will be this number there, if not more, for at least five years, and perhaps twenty-five years, as the pay-dirt extends to a much greater depth than at any other previously-discovered deposit. At least three buckets a day would be used for each person; anyhow, an aggregate of 50,000 a day, which would make an income alone of over £100 a day. Secondly, from water sold for mining purposes. As soon as a miner finds out that by using water at say 2s. a day, he can dispense with four laborers that cost him 12s. a day, and do the same amount of work *much better*, he will most undoubtedly purchase the water, thus giving an income of £200 a day to the stockholders of the water company; and, lastly, the immense advantage to the farms, the owners of which would be willing to pay a good round sum for irrigating water (one farmer offered £1,500 for a running stream of three inches to be taken from the reservoir). There is no doubt but that water-works carried on as above described would pay for themselves in less than two months after they had been laid down; and they could be laid down and put in working order in four months from the time that the order was sent to Europe for the material. The greatest cost of the whole affair would be transportation from the South African port to the fields, which alone would be about £4,000.

The other or cheaper plan of procuring water, but rather uncertain, would be to sink artesian wells; but the objection to this is the uncertainty of getting sufficient water for drinking purposes only, and the uncertainty of cost. The last suggestion that I have to make is starting vegetable gardens. Now, a Californian would get about twenty acres of land from some " chuckle-headed " Dutchman, and plant cabbages, cauliflowers, tomatoes, onions, etc., and make his everlasting dividend therefrom. J. L. B.

N. B.—The above is not particularly for the benefit of the speculator, but if carried out will benefit the miner much.

GEOLOGICAL FEATURES.

A correspondent, writing from Hopetown on the 26th of last month, says:

"What is the real diamond matrix? has been asked over and over again in the diamondiferous tracts of Brazil and India. They have been found imbedded in a micaceous sandstone in Brazil, and in a conglomerate sandstone of India, but neither of these is believed to be the ultimate matrix. It may be that a region which has undergone no changes since the secondary geological epoch, except those of gradual and uniform denudation, like South Africa, may, by ultimate investigation, solve the problem. At all events, I do not believe that the diamonds have been carried down by the Vaal. The Vaal region, I feel persuaded, has been the theater of diamond formation. The component rocks represented in the water-worn pebbles are from the strata and formations of the Vaal—and why not the diamonds?

"This is not the place to enter upon any purely geological discussion. I can not go into details involving the use of geological terminology in a popular newspaper, and therefore what I have said must suffice. One thing, however, may be said in dismissing the subject, that the geology of the Vaal region is altogether different from the secondary and trappen formations of the colony. When the traveler passes through the Free State by Fauresmith, he has the tabular mountains and spitzkops, so common and all-prevailing in South Africa, till he arrives within a few hours' distance of the Vaal. A manifest change sets in, and for miles on miles there is a luxuriant and undulating plain, almost undisturbed by any hills. He feels that there is a break in the structure of the country. When he comes to the Vaal, an entirely different landscape appears before him. The perpetual greenstone porphyries of the colony have vanished, and genuine basalt makes its appearance. This basalt he finds protruding through conglomerate and amygdaloid trap. Glittering pebbles of every form and color glisten at his feet, and he feels indeed that he is in a new region.

"It might be considered desirable that I should give some opinion as to the exact nature of the gravelly mass in which diamonds are more abundantly found. I was careful to question the diggers on this subject, and as a matter of course got very variable information. Some prefer the summits of the kopies rather than the sides, and this opinion is supported by some show of reason, as extensive washing by rain and surface water must carry away the accumulation of gravel from the slopes. But surely the kloofs filled with sand must have under the surface the greater part of the alluvium of the sides. There is no attempt made to penetrate through this sand to the gravel underneath, as yet, by the diggers, and, indeed, their mining is altogether surface work and mere scraping, to what it ought to be. The time will come when the kloofs and hollows will be dug into and searched, and, I believe, with success.

"In regard to the constituent stones of good diamondiferous gravel, satisfactory information cannot be got. Some diggers prefer a light-colored and sparkling gravel; others, again, are greatly in favor of dark, pebbly soil. Diggers generally eschew gravel with quartz fragments (not waterworn) in it. Rotten ironstone pebbles (basalt) are considered a favorable sign. For many reasons, which I cannot discuss in this letter, I am inclined to think that the best indications are garnets (what diggers style rubies) and peridot (a blue, transparent crystal).

"One point, and I must conclude this letter. The tops of the kopies considerably above the present water-level are mentioned above as having alluvial soil, consisting of thoroughly worn and rounded pebbles. A casual observer will quickly perceive that there have been upheavals, and probably successive, everywhere. The basalt of the summits has wedge-shaped crevices, wide at the top and narrowing downward. Forming at one time the bottom of the river, the kopies have been raised, and the alluvial gravel has fallen into the interstices to some extent, the greater part remaining as a cover to the kopies, or rather appearing now as a sort of matrix in which the angular blocks of basalt are imbedded."

A SPLENDID COLLECTION OF DIAMONDS.

After a five months' absence, Mr. Jerome L. Babe, the well-known representative in this colony of the Winchester Repeating Rifle Company, has returned to Capetown from the diamond fields, where he has been singularly successful both in finding and purchasing diamonds. During his stay at the fields he exported to England and America over fifteen hundred diamonds, of which one hundred were as large as twenty-seven carats, and the smallest ten. He has brought with him 275 picked diamonds, which are said to be the finest collection that has ever been seen in this town. They are exhibited in a little glass-covered case, and the singular brilliancy and perfect shape of all the gems are remarkable. They are complete octahedrons, and one of them, of eight carats, is, perhaps, of its size, the most perfect gem that has been found at the fields. These he intends taking with him to America.

Mr. Babe, in leaving this colony, will have the satisfaction of being one of the most successful of those who have visited the diamond fields of South Africa. In addition to this, all the arms imported under his direction have been disposed of in the colony. Mr. Babe is brimful of racy stories of "the diamondiferous regions," and his experience will not deter his countrymen from giving us a look up.

It is not at all unlikely, if Mr. Babe's other engagements do not deter him, that he will give during the ensuing winter a series of illustrated lectures in the chief cities of the United States. He takes home with him sketches of the diamond country, the camps, and the mode of life of the diggers, and he has specimens of soil and gravel. These lectures will do more to give the people of America a correct estimate of our fields than anything that has been said or written about them yet. A casket of diamonds, valued at £5,000, will be one of the great attractions of these lectures.—*Capetown paper.*

THE NEW STORES.

Corner of Adderley and Hout Sts.,
CAPETOWN.

S. R. Stuttaford & Co.,

Drapers, Hosiers, Hatters, Haberdashers,

Cloth and Carpet Warehousemen,

Are receiving per each Mail Steamer

NEW GOODS,

And always keep in Stock a Superior Assortment of Gentlemen's Silk and Felt Hats; also, a large supply of Cloths, Coatings, Angolas, Tweeds, and Doe-skins; White Shirts, Flannel Shirts, Collars, Neck-Ties, Scarfs, Braces, Pocket-Handkerchiefs, Dress and Colored Kid Gloves, Dog-skin and Tilbury Driving Gloves, Umbrellas, Carpet and Leather Bags, Solid Leather Portmanteaus, Socks, Hosiery, Towels, Cotton, Merino, and Lamb's-wool Pants and Under-Vests; Traveling Rugs, Black, Brown, Drab, and California-color Cords and Mole-skins.

LADIES' AND CHILDREN'S UNDER-CLOTHING;

Stays, Jackets, Mantles, Straw Goods, Millinery. Shawls and Dress Materials in great variety. Silks, Satins, and Velvets, in Black and Colored, in well-assorted qualities.

FAMILY MOURNING.

A good assortment of Blankets, Counterpanes, Sheetings, Table Damask, Carpets, Floor Cloth, Cloth and Damask Table Covers, Muslin Curtains, Muslin, Duck, and Wagon Canvas, Drills, American Leathers, Cart Trimmings.

Ladies' and Children's Gloves, Hosiery, Lace, Ribbons, Buttons, Trimmings. Haberdashery of all descriptions.

Samples of any description of Cut Material forwarded to any part of the Colony. It will be to the interest of our country friends to forward their orders direct; by so doing they will be enabled to obtain, per post-cart or transport wagon,

First-class Articles at very Reduced Prices.

Note the Address—

S. R. STUTTAFORD & CO.,
ADDERLEY STREET AND HOUT STREET,
CAPETOWN.

J. KURELLA,

No. 16 CASTLE ST., CAPETOWN,

EXPORTER OF

COLONIAL PRODUCE,

Buys Rough Diamonds at highest market rates, and makes liberal advances on Produce consigned to his Agents,

Messrs. ROSING, MELCHER'S,

Billiter Square, London, England.

VAN DER BYLT & CO.,

39 St. George's Street,

CAPETOWN,

Merchants & Commission Agents.

ORDERS FOR PURCHASE OF

DIAMONDS, WOOL, SKINS,

and other Colonial Produce suitable for the American market, promptly attended to.

Liberal advances made on Consignments.

REFEREES:

Messrs. REYNOLDS & CUSHMAN, New York,
Messrs. CHALMERS, GUTHRIE & CO.,
9 Idol Lane, London.

TAYLOR, KEMP & COMPANY,

GENERAL

AND

COMMISSION MERCHANTS,

AND

SHIPPING AND INSURANCE AGENTS,

PORT ELIZABETH, ALGOA BAY,

CAPE OF GOOD HOPE.

Boston and New York: ISAAC TAYLOR.

CENTRAL HOTEL,

DU TOIT'S PAN.

MESSRS. BENNING & MARTIN

Beg to announce their having opened the LEVIATHAN HOTEL, in the most central position of DU TOIT'S PAN, where the weary traveler will find every comfort. Good Single and Double-Bedded Rooms, spacious Dining Saloon, replete with every comfort and luxury.

Brilliant Bar, with best of everything drinkable.

Luxurious Card and Lounging Rooms, Lavatories, etc., and a good staff of attendants on man and beast.

THE WHOLE SUPERINTENDED BY THE PROPRIETORS,

BENNING & MARTIN,

Late of King Williamstown and Pniel.

ALFRED DOCKS,

TABLE BAY, CAPE OF GOOD HOPE,

INAUGURATED BY

H. R. H. THE DUKE OF EDINBURGH,

On the 11th July, 1870,

Are now Open to the Trade of the World.

They consist of an INNER BASIN of ten acres, with a depth of 24 feet low water, with an entrance 100 feet wide, and an OUTER BASIN of six acres; the whole protected by a BREAKWATER extending 1,000 feet into the Bay.

The Dues for Vessels entering the Docks are 6*d.* per ton register for one month, and 1*d.* per ton per week afterward.

There are

No Harbor, Light, or any other Dues Chargeable on Shipping Frequenting the Port.

In the Inner Basin of the Dock there is a PATENT SLIP, capable of taking up vessels of 1,500 tons burden, and the charges are:

For vessels of 50 tons and under, £15 for ten days, and £3 per day after.

Vessels over 50 tons, taken up for repairs, 7*s.* 6*d.* per register ton for ten days, and £6 per day after.

Iron vessels taken up for cleaning and painting only, 5*s.* per register ton for ten days, and £6 for every day after.

Steamers charged according to their gross tonnage.

The Ten Days are Exclusive of Sundays.

The days of taking up and launching are reckoned as one.

The Purest Water is Delivered on Board of Vessels in the Docks at Three Shillings per Ton.

By order of the Board.

JNO. SAUNDERS,
Secretary.

Table Bay Harbor Commission Office,
CAPETOWN, *July,* 1870.

DIAMONDS,
Rough and Cut,
BOUGHT AND SOLD
OR
SET TO ORDER
BY
G. A. BOETGER,
Watchmaker, Jeweler, and Optician,
7 SHORTMARKET STREET,
Opposite the Central Hotel,
CAPETOWN.

G. A. B.'s long acquaintance with this Colony enables him to direct his particular attention to Importing that class of Articles which are best adapted for general wear in this climate, and begs to inform his Customers and the Public that he has always in Stock

Gold and Silver English and Geneva
WATCHES,
Fine Gold Jewelry
OF EVERY DESCRIPTION AND LATEST DESIGNS.

Diamond Scales and Weights, Magnifying Glasses, Emery Files, Colored and Plain Spectacles, Goggles, Telescopes, Field and Night Glasses, Compasses and Nautical Instruments, etc.

DIAMONDS SENT TO EUROPE FOR CUTTING.

Guarantee Given for every Watch Sold or Repaired.

☞ All new work and Repairs intrusted to G. A. B.'s care are executed on the Premises.

Orders from the Fields punctually attended to in the shortest possible Time.

BY SPECIAL APPOINTMENT
TO H. R. H. DUKE OF EDINBURGH.

JAMES LONG,
TOBACCONIST,
No. 1
SHORTMARKET STREET
CAPETOWN.

TWO DOORS FROM CENTRAL HOTEL.

EMIL BURMESTER,
23 Adderley St. & 2 Shortmarket St.,
JEWELER, WATCHMAKER, AND OPTICIAN,
DEALER IN
Photographic and Fancy Goods,

Has always on hand a large stock of the choicest of fine Gold Jewelry, Silver Cups, Inkstands, Snuff Boxes, Silver Electro-plated Ware, Cutlery, Perfumery and Scented Soap, Telescopes and Opera-Glasses, Musical Boxes, Diamond Scales, Microscopes, Emery Files for testing Diamonds, Gold and Silver Watches, and Clocks.

E. B. being a Practical Optician, would recommend parties whose sight is failing to call at his establishment for

SPECTACLES,

as they can be manufactured to suit every sight. Also, colored glass Spectacles for the Fields.

Photographs of Capetown, Diamond Fields, and the different Native Tribes. *Diamonds, Old Gold, and Silver Bought.*

23 Adderley Street and 2 Shortmarket Street.

QUICK PASSAGE
TO THE
DIAMOND FIELDS.
CAPE AND NATAL STEAM NAVIGATION CO.

This Company starts a Steamer on the first of each Month. The Port of Departure is LONDON. The Vessel calls at DARTMOUTH to embark Mails and Passengers.

The Steamers are First-Class ones of 2,000 tons and 600 Horse-Power. The Passenger Accommodation is

UNRIVALED BY ANY BOAT IN THE TRADE.

FARES:

Chief Cabin..........30 Guineas | 2d Class...............20 Guineas

The Agents in England are

Messrs. PAYNE & CO.,
LEADENHALL STREET,

AND AT THE CAPE,

W. DICKSON & CO.

THE CAPE AND NATAL
STEAMSHIP COMPANY

DISPATCH THEIR

STEAMERS FROM LONDON MONTHLY,

CALLING AT

CAPETOWN, **PORT ELIZABETH,**
MOSSEL BAY, **NATAL,** **EAST LONDON.**

AFFORDING MOST DESIRABLE OPPORTUNITIES FOR PARTIES

PROCEEDING

TO ALL PORTS OF THE COLONY,

EN ROUTE TO THE

DIAMOND FIELDS
OF
SOUTH AFRICA.

APPLICATION IN LONDON TO

G. H. PAYNE & CO.

AT THE HEAD OFFICE, 117 LEADENHALL STREET,

OR TO

ANDERSON & MURISON.

Masonic Hotel,
CAPETOWN.

THIS IS THE

First-Class Hotel of Capetown.

Its position is central, and within two minutes' walk of the principal Landing Wharf.

No Hotel in Capetown is possessed of the advantages such as those secured for the

MASONIC.

The Cuisine is Unequaled.

SKILLED WAITERS ARE ENGAGED,

And every Attention is shown.

THE LIQUORS ARE OF THE BEST,

AND THE

CHARGES ARE MODERATE.

NEWSPAPERS, PERIODICALS, AND MAGAZINES

RECEIVED BY EVERY MAIL.

Passengers arriving in the Colony should not fail to engage Apartments at this Hotel.

MASONIC HOTEL,
DARLING STREET,
CAPETOWN.

R. M. ROSS,
IRONMONGERY STORES,

Strand Street and St. George's Street,

CAPETOWN, SOUTH AFRICA.

Importer of British and Foreign
MANUFACTURES IN HARDWARE,

HAS CONSTANTLY IN STOCK

AGRICULTURAL AND GARDEN IMPLEMENTS,
Machinists' Tools of Every Description,

Colormens' Materials, Oils, Paints, Varnish, Brushware, etc.

Furnishing Ironmongery, Hollow-ware, Enamel-ware, Cutlery, Albataware Cutlery,

Tinware, Washing Basins, Baths, Tea and Coffee-Pots,

FIRE-PROOF SAFES,

GUNPOWDER, SHOT, CAPS, SHOT-POUCHES, Etc., Etc.

Merchants and Country Dealers Supplied at the Lowest Wholesale Rates.

G. S. HOLMES & CO.,
AMERICAN SHIPPING
AND
COMMISSION MERCHANTS.

Agents for the
UNITED STATES BOARDS OF UNDERWRITERS.

Agents for the
NEW BEDFORD AND NEW LONDON WHALEMEN,

CAPETOWN, C. G. H.

REFERENCES:

Boston: Messrs. W. F. Weld & Co., Messrs. H. W. Peabody & Co.
New York: Messrs. W. W. De Forest & Co., Frederick Baker, Esq.

Messrs. Holmes & Co. have been Established here over Thirty Years, and are thoroughly acquainted with the Business and Resources of the Colony. Large Stocks of

AMERICAN IMPORTS
ALWAYS ON HAND.

☞ Consignments or Orders for the Purchase of Produce will receive Prompt and Careful Attention.

LIBERAL ADVANCES MADE ON DIAMONDS.

THE STANDARD BANK
OF
BRITISH SOUTH AFRICA.
(LIMITED.)

NOMINAL CAPITAL,
Three Million Pounds (£3,000,000) Sterling.

HEAD OFFICE,
10 CLEMENTS LANE, LOMBARD ST., LONDON, E. C.

London Bankers:
BANK OF ENGLAND, ALLIANCE BANK.

BRANCHES IN SOUTH AFRICA:

Aliwal North, Beaufort West, Capetown, Colesberg, Cradock, Durban (Natal), Graham'stown, King William's Town, Klip Drift (DIAMOND FIELDS), Mossel Bay, Pieter Maritz burg (Natal), Port Elizabeth, Richmond, Somerset East, Uitenhage, Victoria West.

General Manager in South Africa—ROBERT STEWART, Esq.

Agents—British and Colonial.

NATIONAL PROVINCIAL BANK OF ENGLAND.
COMMERCIAL BANK OF SCOTLAND.
NORTH OF SCOTLAND BANKING COMPANY
ULSTER BANKING COMPANY.
HIBERNIAN JOINT-STOCK BANK.
ORIENTAL BANK CORPORATION.
CHARTERED MERCANTILE BANK OF INDIA, LONDON, AND CHINA.
UNION BANK OF AUSTRALIA (Australia and New Zealand).
BANK OF NEW ZEALAND.

Agents—Foreign.

In United States of America:

NEW YORK..Messrs. HOWLAND & ASPINWALL.
BOSTON......Messrs. WARREN & CO.

In Brazils—LONDON AND BRAZILIAN BANK.

Every description of Banking business connected with South Africa or elsewhere conducted on the most favorable terms.

Undertakes the realization of Diamonds and other precious Stones, in any of the chief markets of the world which the owners may select, accounting for the proceeds, *in gold*, at the Diamond Fields, at any of the Branches in South Africa, at the Head Office in London, or elsewhere.

Persons proceeding to South Africa, or having payments to make there, can obtain *Drafts or Letters of Credit* on any of the Branches there, either by direct application to the Head Office in London, or through any of the Agents of the Bank.

JEROME L. BABE,

DEALER IN

Rough and Cut

DIAMONDS.

Mr. Babe goes to Europe four times a year, purchases Rough Diamonds from the

South African Diamond Mines,

has them cut, and is thus enabled to supply the American Trade with

THE

Finest Diamonds

AT THE LOWEST RATES.

Address to
3,217 Sansom Street,
Philadelphia, Pa.

TO THE DIAMOND FIELDS AND BACK
IN
EIGHTEEN DAYS.

CAPE OF GOOD HOPE
Inland Transport Company.
(*LIMITED*).

The Company's Wagons, for the Conveyance of Passengers and Parcels, leave Capetown by the shortest route for the Pniel Diamond Fields by the 7.16 Train every Thursday and Saturday Morning, returning to Capetown on the Monday fortnight following by the 6.30 A.M. Train from Wellington.

To enable Passengers to reach the Fields in the time named, continuous relays of Cattle are employed.

Refreshments may be obtained at any of the Stopping Places **at very reasonable Rates.**

FARES:

To Beaufort West	£5
To Victoria West	6
To Hopetown	9
To the Diamond Fields	12

40lb. Luggage allowed. Extra Luggage by Special Agreement.

Packages and Parcels are conveyed to
- Beaufort or Victoria West, at 6d. per pound.
- To Hopetown, at 9d. per pound.
- To the Diamond Fields, at 1s. 3d. per pound.

The Vehicles may be inspected by intending Passengers; and any further information, either as regards Time-tables or Intermediate Fares, obtained by application to the undersigned. Information can also be obtained at the Commercial Exchange, or at the Railway Station, Capetown.

Passengers and Parcels are booked at the Office of the Company, Grave Street, one door from Darling Street, Capetown, Cape of Good Hope. Information can also be obtained at the Commercial Exchange and the Railway Station in Capetown. Passengers' Luggage must be delivered and weighed on or before Wednesday Evening at five o'clock.

THOMAS GARDNER,
Secretary.

ISAAC SONNENBERG & CO.,

DIRECT IMPORTERS OF

London & American Manufactures,

PROVISIONS AND MINING TOOLS.

Always on hand,

SCOTCH CARTS, CRADLES, and the right sort of PICKAXES and SHOVELS.

Parties going to the DIAMOND FIELDS will do well to FIT themselves out here in JACOBSDAL, as it is only thirty-six miles from the MAIN DIGGINGS, and goods bought here will be forwarded with our own wagons to the Diggings, FREE OF CHARGE.

ALL MINING IMPLEMENTS

have been personally selected by our Mr. ISAAC SONNENBERG, who has had seventeen years' experience in Mining in California, Nevada, Idaho, and Montana Territory, U. S. America.

Give us a call as you pass through, as it is the nearest route to the Diggings.

Any information about New Camps, and so forth given *without charge.*

AGENTS FOR PORT ELIZABETH AND QUEENSTOWN PASSENGER CARTS;

And DAILY COMMUNICATION with the DIAMOND FIELDS, JACOBSDAL, O. F. State.

January, 1871.

ISAAC SONNENBERG & CO

Branch Houses at
DU TOIT'S PAN AND THE NEW RUSHES.

Winchester Repeating
FIRE-ARMS,

16 SHOTS IN 10 SECONDS,

OR

30 Shots a Minute as a Single Loader.

THE BEST

Sporting Rifle in the World;

AND THE

BEST DEFENSIVE WEAPON KNOWN.

Metallic Waterproof Cartridges.

Price, from $40 to $100,

ACCORDING TO FINISH.

CARTRIDGES $20 PER 1,000.

Manufactured at New Haven, Conn.

Sold by all Gunsmiths throughout the Union,

AND BY

Messrs. G. S. HOLMES & CO.,

CAPETOWN,

Messrs. TAYLOR, KEMP & CO.,

PORT ELIZABETH,

AND

Messrs. Henderson & Scott,

DURBAN, NATAL.

These Rifles are Universally Used at the

DIAMOND FIELDS.

www.ingramcontent.com/pod-product-compliance
Lightning Source LLC
Chambersburg PA
CBHW031343160426
43196CB00007B/731